The Telegraph

BOOK OF

READERS' LETTERS
FROM THE GREAT WAR

The Telegraph

BOOK OF

READERS' LETTERS
FROM THE GREAT WAR

—◄— EDITED BY —►—
GAVIN FULLER

Aurum
Press

First published in Great Britain
2014 by Aurum Press Ltd
74—77 White Lion Street
Islington
London N1 9PF
www.aurumpress.co.uk

A catalogue record for this book is available from the British Library.

ISBN 978 1 78131 330 5

10 9 8 7 6 5 4 3 2 1
2018 2017 2016 2015 2014

Typeset in Dante by Saxon Graphics Ltd, Derby
Printed by CPI Group (UK) Ltd, Croydon, CR0 4YY

Introduction

The letters published in the *Daily Telegraph* during the First World War tell a different story to the entrenched notion that it was the 'war to end war.' Curiously the battles of the war don't engender a single letter in the newspaper – whether this *omertà* was decided upon as a policy decision by the newspaper or even perhaps the authorities rather than the readers is, alas, one lost in the mists of time, but it does seem remarkable that even events such as the sinking of RMS *Lusitania* did not generate letters of outrage in the newspaper.

Nevertheless the four and a quarter years of conflict meant that the *Telegraph*'s readers found plenty to write about and the paper became host to a number of letters from the great and good – members of the Royal Family, leading politicians and authors all put (or had put on their behalf) pen to paper to the Editor. One thing that is striking when reading through the newspapers of the war is the number of letters asking for donations, whether it be money or other articles; this book could have been filled with the letters from those asking for our readers' assistance, and even as the war drew to a close there were still contributions of this type appearing. In the early days of the war, these letters do make one wonder just how efficiently the supply chain to our armed forces was being organised by the Government; a request for readers to donate field glasses to officers for example, or to supply mufflers for our soldiers, or stockings for our sailors doesn't really reflect well on the powers that be, whilst others cast a sadder light on things.

What our letter writers often do though, is provide another aspect to a country facing a war like none it had fought before, and this throws up a number of questions. For example, 'Just what should our clergymen's response to this situation be?' created a serious debate amongst our readers. The frustrations of men not in the full flush of youth but who wished to do their bit for King and Country are, perhaps unsurprisingly with this newspaper, writ large, as are the grievances with those who are in that flush but not perceived to be doing so. It is prescient that the first letters of the war are concern for the nation's food supply given what was to ensue with the German submarine campaign against our merchant shipping. Some of the letters make one's jaw drop – a canon extolling the joys of the French Riviera or our organ builders arguing that just because there is a war on why should people stop buying their products? And some make one wonder – why on earth would a council deem the lending of fiction from its libraries unsuitable during wartime?

Just as it was a war beyond comprehension on the front line, it was also a war felt and fought on the home front like none before. Collected together for the first time, these letters paint a portrait of a society scarred by tragedy, guilt and grief, but also of a country battling to give their all and to 'do their bit'. Most of all they reveal a nation joining together as they try and come to terms with a war that would alter the course of their lives forever.

Gavin Fuller
August 2014

4 August 1914

CARE OF NATION'S FOOD

SIR – At a time of national crisis, when less than ever can we calculate what may be the requirements of the future, it behoves all patriotic people to take the utmost care and thought that nothing, however small, which may be of eventual service to the people is neglected.

In view of this we venture to suggest that the multitude of small unused or uncropped plots of ground should at once be planted with such food plants as it is possible to sow at this season of the year. It is too late for corn of any kind, too late for potatoes. Turnips, however, should do well after the rains of the last few days. Turnip-rooted beet, carrots and onions – of suitable varieties – would in a favourable autumn yield fair-sized bulbs.

Every day is of importance, as the time is not far distant when vegetative growth will cease for the year.

There are also in almost all gardens beds surplus stock of cabbage and savoy plants. Let them be planted out as far as can be, and let the remainder be at once given to cottagers and others who will do likewise.

These may seem trifling matters, but the day may come when trifles count, and from personal observation of the enormous number of unused corners and odd plots of land, we are convinced that the total increase of foodstuffs would be by no means small if everyone with land would do as we suggest.

It should also be impressed on farmers not to leave vacant any land that may be profitably used in the manner we are urging.

W. Wilks, Secretary, RHS
Frederick Keeble, Director, RHS Gardens, Wisley
Royal Horticultural Society, Vincent Square, Westminster, S.W.

———

7 August 1914

CIVILIANS AND THE HARVEST

SIR – All patriotic men desire at this critical period to do their duty to their country. It is a mistake to suppose that military service is the only, or in many cases the best, means of carrying out such duty. There is at the moment no greater national need than the speedy harvesting, without interruption, of the present bountiful crops of wheat and other cereals in this country, and the resowing of the land with similar crops as soon as possible. In some districts the shortage of agricultural labour is considerable, and is daily increasing. This is due partly to the calling up for military service of Reservists and the embodiment of the Territorials, and partly to the non-arrival of the Irish labourers who usually visit England at this time to help with the corn harvest. The difficulty is accentuated by the impressment for military requirements of many of the farm horses. Local labour exchanges are being instructed by the Board of Trade to help the farmers at this crisis as much as possible, and the Board of Agriculture is sending a circular on this subject to local chambers of agriculture throughout the kingdom. May I suggest that civilians, regardless of all social distinctions, who are at present unable to serve their country in other ways should, through the nearest labour exchange or otherwise, offer forthwith their patriotic assistance, either continuously for the next three weeks or alternatively during the weekends, in the process of getting in the harvest?

Yours faithfully,

Charles Bathurst
House of Commons

THE GERMAN EMBASSY

American's Strong Protest

SIR – I today have addressed to the American ambassador a note, a copy of which I beg to enclose to you. The matter is one of such moment that it ought, I feel, to be given currency in your columns.

Sincerely yours,

S. Gross Horwitz
London

TO HIS EXCELLENCY THE
AMERICAN AMBASSADOR

MY DEAR SIR – I note with deep regret and concern that the affairs of the German Embassy have been taken over by you. A more unfortunate diplomatic performance it is difficult for me to conceive. At a time when all the nations of the earth – the United States in particular – have been engaged in promoting the cause of peace, the German bravo privately has been engaged in hatching the means of profiting by their pacific policies. The world is now awake, and realises that the disturber of the repose of all men, this German blusterer, drunk with self-infatuation, would sacrifice all interests to his own. Millions already are sufferers as the result of his unprovoked iniquities. Locked up in London, I, an American citizen, find myself unable to obtain even funds; thousands of others the same. Bankruptcy upon vast masses of beings already has fallen, and upon vast masses more must bankruptcy fall unless the course of this latter-day barbarian promptly be arrested. That, in such circumstances, the American nation should, directly or indirectly, give sanction to the German cause by lending itself to the transaction in London of German affairs is pollution to the American name.

In a just cause the law of nations sanctions such a course, but not in an infamous one. Far from it. International ethics justify, on the contrary, a banding together of all nations against an imperious brigand, bent upon subjugating all people to his will. The country which has deputed you hither, he has insulted equally with all other countries. He has, in other words, caused an incalculable number of human beings throughout the world to suffer in an infinite variety of ways. It, therefore, is, I feel, incumbent upon some American citizens sternly to protect against the action which the American Embassy has taken. Hence do I beg leave to request in my own name, and in the name of hundreds of thousands of other Americans, I feel sure, that you will at once notify to the German people that you are unable in any capacity to act for them.

With profound assurances of regard,

I am, dear Sir,

Sincerely yours,

S. Gross Horwitz
Berkeley Hotel, Piccadilly, W.

---

8 August 1914

COUNTRY HOUSES

Use as Hospitals

SIR – There must be many who, like myself, are willing to lend their country houses on the east and south-east coast of Great Britain, and in the neighbourhood of London, for hospital purposes in the present crisis.

There will certainly be an influx of sick and wounded to this country within a short time, and we must make every possible effort to accommodate them under the most comfortable conditions.

For the purpose of converting the houses into hospitals and convalescent homes expert advice is advisable, and will those who are prepared to offer their houses on these lines write to me with full particulars of their houses and accommodation at 26 Victoria Street, London S.W., where I have made arrangements for all inquiries to be attended to by those who are fully competent to do so.

I feel certain a central bureau of this description would considerably facilitate the medical departments of the Admiralty and of the War Office, and enable them to get a list of people willing to lend their houses at the shortest notice, and, in addition, enable those who wish to help in this way to do so in the most efficient manner.

Yours faithfully,

Sutherland
Dunrobin Castle, Sutherland

10 August 1914

HOSPITAL FOR ALLIES

Lady Sarah Wilson's Plea

SIR – As a soldier's wife – one of the many in England today who have a smile on their lips while fear grips their hearts – I make an appeal for a fund to organise and equip a base or stationary hospital for English, French and Belgian soldiers, to be established at a convenient spot on the Continent, the locality of which would be determined by the progress of hostilities.

Naturally, plans for the moment must be obscure, but it would seem that it is at present intended to bring disabled soldiers back to England for hospital treatment. When I was in South Africa during the Boer War, I constantly witnessed the arrival of the injured after an engagement, and I can only say, with such scenes vividly before me, that I am haunted day and night by the idea of those grievously wounded having to face additional discomforts in the shape of a crowded ship, of a rough sea. I am not referring to those slightly wounded.

We know full well that the Government arrangements for the sick and wounded will be in every way as efficient as the expeditionary force itself; but in a struggle of this kind, when all available hospital space will be taxed to its utmost limits, it would be an inestimable boon to the Army base hospitals to have some cases – perhaps the most severe ones – taken off their hands.

It should be called to mind that during the Boer War over 20,000 patients were treated in a supplementary hospital. I allude to the Imperial Yeomanry Hospital organised by my sister, the late Countess Howe, and the late Lady Chesham.

I propose to form a small committee and to run the hospital under the auspices of the Red Cross Society.

I further hope to engage the best available surgeons and nurses.

If the public will entrust me with their money, I will guarantee that, as far as energy and hard work will go, the soldiers will get full benefit for every penny subscribed.

He gives twice who gives quickly! Surely this were never more true than now, for seldom, if ever, have our dear ones been so suddenly called to the battlefield.

Subscriptions and any gifts in kind will be gratefully received and acknowledged by me at 16 Grosvenor Street, W., which the Hon. Mrs George Keppel has generously offered as an office for the proposed fund.

Yours faithfully,

Sarah Wilson

12 August 1914

GERMAN TREATMENT OF ENGLISH LADIES

SIR – I have seen it stated that the Germans have treated with courtesy and kindness English travellers who happened to be in their country on the outbreak of war. The narration of my own unfortunate experiences may serve to convince your readers how different are the real facts.

On Saturday, 1 August, a party, consisting of a German officer, who had permission to escort me as far as the Dutch frontier, my chauffeur, and myself, left Homburg in a motor car, intending to make for Cologne. We travelled on the right bank of the Rhine as far as Rüdesheim, and took the ferry boat across to Bingerbrüch, where we were turned back. There were pickets everywhere, and whenever our car was stopped, which happened frequently, people crowded round it. We were not actually molested, but the attitude of the inhabitants was distinctly hostile, and they made use of many uncomplimentary expressions.

We returned to Rüdesheim, and made progress as far as Braubach. There we were met by a hostile crowd, and were forced to go before the Burgomaster, who told us he had been informed by telephone that we were spies. This was not pleasant news, because we had heard that a good many alleged spies had been arrested, and some of them had been shot almost immediately.

Finally, after our luggage had been searched, we were taken by train under military escort to Coblenz. Next morning we were required to present ourselves at the prefecture, and after telephoning in various directions the officials permitted us to depart.

Returning to Braubach, we recovered our motor car, and succeeded in reaching Cleves about ten o'clock the same night. Next morning we resumed our journey, but were stopped on the German side of the Dutch frontier, just beside the barrier, and rigorously searched. After being kept waiting for five hours in a village street, we were informed that the road by which we had come was closed to motors, and two soldiers were told to accompany us to Wesel.

On arriving at Wesel we were instructed to drive to the citadel, and, to our extreme astonishment, the officer in charge ordered us to be thrown into prison. I was put in a dirty cell, bad enough for the worst criminal, and as a special concession I was given a cane chair to sit upon. The weather was very hot, and the want of air in the cell caused me much physical distress. After a couple of hours or so the sergeant yielded to my earnest entreaties that I should be given better quarters, and conveyed me to the rooms occupied by himself and his wife.

A Military Court

Next morning I was summoned to appear before a military court consisting of three officers, and was severely catechised, my answers being taken down in writing. Afterwards my imprisonment was not so rigorous, as I was allowed to stay in a big room guarded by a sentry with a loaded rifle. In the afternoon the wife of my officer friend arrived from Düsseldorf, and visited the citadel to intercede on my behalf.

However, the authorities would not release me until a telegram came from the British Ambassador, about half-past nine in the evening, after which both my chauffeur and myself were set free. My German companion was detained until the following morning. In the meantime I heard from the wife that he had been given a high appointment on the general staff of one of the army corps.

Thanks to his good offices I afterwards obtained a pass for myself and my chauffeur, as well as permission to buy petrol. My troubles were not yet at an end, but it will suffice to say that, escorted by four soldiers in a motor car, I at length reached the frontier at Gronaü. Here I thankfully bade goodbye to German territory,

I was received most kindly by the Dutch officials, who provided me with a pass to Rotterdam, where I spent the night. The next day I got another pass from the British Legation at The Hague, and in the afternoon I motored as far as Bergen-op-Zoom, where the car was obliged to be put in an open truck. Sitting in the car, my chauffeur and I accomplished the journey to Flushing in six hours. The steamer was waiting already, and I was thankful to have a good night's rest. Next day the ship left at eleven o'clock, and I reached Folkestone at seven o'clock, where I was met by my husband.

Yours, &c.,
Mary Stewart Mackenzie.
47 Berkeley Square, W.

———

13 August 1914

CIVILIAN NATIONAL RESERVE

SIR – A movement is on foot by which men who can find no other way of serving their country shall form themselves into local bodies which shall drill and learn to shoot, organising themselves and forming a reserve without worrying the authorities in any way.

In this small town we have raised 200 such men, who are hard at work drilling and at the butts. We have had 250 applications from other centres for details as to our method of organisation.

I should be happy to send these to anyone who desires it. No one can tell the course of this war, nor predict how far in a few months' time the existence of some hundreds of thousands of additional who have had some elementary military training may affect the situation.

Yours faithfully,

Arthur Conan Doyle
Windlesham, Crowborough, Sussex

14 August 1914

CALL TO YACHTSMEN

Volunteers Wanted

SIR – My steam yacht is being fitted out for the purpose of serving in every possible way the work for the transport of wounded refugees. I am running her myself with a captain, an engineer and a pilot. All other members of the crew are volunteers. I am wanting gentlemen with £300 each who will volunteer to complete the crew. The call is urgent, and surely there are many yachtsmen who are prevented from serving their country in other ways, but who can give their services and a little of their incomes for such a cause.

We cannot, and must not, wait until the last minute. The motto for every man and woman in England today is, 'Be prepared!' I therefore ask those men who have not gone to the front to assist me as far as in their power lies, and to do that promptly, without delay, bearing in mind that every hour counts now.

All contributions will he gratefully received by Miss Borthwick, 83 Pall Mall, S.W.

Yours truly,

Jessica Borthwick
83 Pall Mall, S.W.

CARE OF THE WOUNDED

Evils of Overlapping
Lord Rothschild's Appeal

SIR – The vast, and, indeed, astounding number of offers of help which continue to be made day by day to the British Red Cross Society show – if any such demonstration were needed – the kind-heartedness of the whole British people, and their intense eagerness to be of some assistance to our gallant soldiers and sailors; but kind-heartedness and anxiety to help are of little avail, unless they are organised and applied – not as sentiment dictates, but as the actual need demands.

We are threatened with the same confusion that so crippled the Red Cross effort in the South African War, with the same evils of overlapping, of unco-ordinated and disunited work. Private houses are being turned into hospitals and convalescent homes, without reference to any organising body and without regard to any rational scheme. Nurses are engaged who may never be required in the particular place allotted to them, while, worst of all, stores of surgical material are being hoarded up in scores of houses to such an extent that the market is seriously depleted. Ladies are starting independent base-hospitals of their own, and are appealing for funds for their maintenance.

Surgeons and nurses are struggling to reach the front without any organisation, and without definite orders or definite plans. All these efforts are most kindly meant, but they are producing an amount of disorder and waste of personnel and equipment which is to be deplored.

Need For More Money

The British Red Cross Society has already a number of beds at its disposal which, while probably sufficient to meet the coming need, can be almost indefinitely expanded on efficient and economic lines. The organisation of the society extends throughout the whole country, and beds can be provided in sufficient number as and when they are required.

The British Red Cross Society is working in close harmony with the St John Ambulance Association, and no one can dispute that these two bodies are competent to deal promptly, efficiently and economically with the intending need, colossal as it is, if only they are supplied with sufficient funds. All but the clerical work of administration of the Red Cross Society is carried out by trained volunteers, every department is in charge of competent experts, while offices and storerooms are provided, free of all cost, by the generosity of the Duke of Devonshire.

In every detail the society keeps in close touch with the War Office and Admiralty, to whom, and to whom alone, they look for instructions as to where help is needed, and of what kind it should be. The expenses for equipment, for personnel and for supplies must needs be heavy, but those who come to our aid have the assurance that the funds subscribed will not be scattered in private enterprises, but will be employed to the direct and prompt relief of the sick and wounded. At this moment – so many are the calls upon the charitable – the Red Cross Society of this country is in need of means to carry out, on business lines, a mission of mercy, the organisation of which has been the deliberate work of years.

Yours faithfully,

Rothschild, Chairman, Council of the British Red Cross Society

———

WAR AND OPERA

The Carl Rosa Company

SIR – In the exceptional circumstances may I beg the hospitality of your columns?

When the appalling news of the war burst on us, naturally our first impulse was to cancel our forthcoming tour, or, at least, the first portion of it. On reflection, however, the thought of over a hundred artists being thrown out of work to their great distress, and the distress of those dependent on them, and the great difficulty of getting fresh engagements just at present, made us reconsider the matter, and we decided to make a start in the ordinary manner.

The expenses of an opera company are, however, so very great that it will be impossible to continue if business is very bad for long. Would you permit me to state that we are at the Coronet Theatre, 7 September; Kennington, 14 September; and the

Marlborough Theatre, 21 September, and I would be most grateful if those members of the public who intend to be present would notify their intention to the respective theatre or myself. We could then get an inkling as to what would be our fate.

The Carl Rosa Opera Company might almost be called a national institution. It has been in existence forty-three years, and is the oldest theatrical enterprise in Great Britain, besides being the oldest English opera company in the world. It has introduced hundreds of great operas and singers to the British public, and I am sure that hundreds and thousands of Britishers all over the world would much regret if it was forced to suspend its operations.

I have just heard that another opera company has cancelled its tour, thus adding to the unemployed.

I am, Sir, yours very truly,

Walter Van Noorden, Managing Director
Carl Rosa Opera Company (Ltd.), 14 and 14a, Wrotham Road, Camden Road, N.W.

REGIMENTAL AGENCY

Princess Louise's Appeal

SIR – At this juncture, when money is being generously subscribed for the assistance of our wounded and invalided soldiers as they return from the war, we desire to commend to the consideration of the public the system of distribution of benefits through the regiments in which the men have served.

Almost every regiment has now its own association providing adequate machinery for giving relief to its old soldiers. The men are personally known in the regiment, and any assistance they may receive from this source in times of distress is not regarded as charity, but as an honourable recognition of their services with the colours.

The Regimental Agency, of which His Majesty the King is patron, is managed by a committee of officers. It acts as the handmaid of the regimental associations. Nine of these associations carry on their work in these offices, whilst others are helped by the Agency in various ways. The Agency also serves as a clearing house, passing on to the regimental associations applications from, or on behalf of, old soldiers, to be dealt with regimentally. Donations sent to us will at once be forwarded to the regiments in which the donors are specially interested.

We further appeal for funds, as also for personal help, for the Regimental Agency itself, to enable us to carry on our work for the regimental associations at a time when a severe strain is made on our resources and most of our helpers have been called off by the war.

Subscriptions and donations should be sent direct to the Regimental Agency, 33 Tothill Street, Westminster, S.W.

Yours faithfully,

Louise, President
Roberts, F.M., Vice-President
Methuen, Vice-Chairman of Council
Claude M. Macdonald, Chairman of Central Committee
The Regimental Agency, 33 Tothill Street, Westminster, S.W.

————

1 September 1914

BRITISH AIRMAN'S GRAVE

SIR – Last week in Belgium I saw a wrecked British aeroplane and beside it the grave of the aviator. At the time I was a prisoner with the Germans, and could not stop or ask questions. Later, with the object of establishing the identity of the aviator, I visited the place. Should after the war the family of the officer desire to remove his body I am writing this that they may know where it is now buried.

The aeroplane fell to the road between Enghien and Ath. Belgians near the place told me the officer was shot down by a column of German infantry, the strength of which column he was evidently trying to discover. The aeroplane was totally destroyed, but on a twisted plate I found the name of an English firm. There were also in the wreck paper forms for making out reports on reconnaissances. There was no writing on these, but the printed matter was in English.

At the head of the grave the Germans had put a wooden cross, on which they had written 'Herr Flier, 22 August 1914'. The Belgians had covered the grave with flowers. It should not be difficult to find. It is on the left-hand side of the road as one walks south from Enghien to Ath in a pear orchard, near a very old red-brick house with a square tower.

One hundred yards south of the grave is a signpost that reads, pointing south, 'Ath – 14 kil.', pointing north, 'Enghien – 5 kil.' Enghien is about thirty kilometres south of Brussels.

I am, yours truly,

Richard Harding Davis, Correspondent, New York Tribune
10 Clarges Street, W.

———

3 September 1914

HELP FOR THE BELGIANS

Great Need of Foodstuffs

SIR – I hesitate again to address you, but, against my own wishes, I am being urged by some of the greatest merchants in England to do so. I cannot appear as a mendicant on behalf of my country. Her actions speak for themselves.

Moreover, Britain has already responded nobly in gifts of money and kind to help those suffering in Belgium. Again, many merchants have already sent me noble gifts; and, moreover, Britain has its own needy calls.

What I am asked to state is that there will very shortly be a great want of foodstuffs in many important places in Belgium, and that the sufferings, not only of the wounded, but of the inhabitants, and especially of little children, will probably be excessive. For these reasons I am told that the great merchants of Britain, who may not already have shown their appreciation of the efforts of Belgium, would be only too willing to make gifts of foodstuffs were transit available. It is believed that an opportunity will very shortly be placed at my disposal whereby foodstuffs in large quantities could be delivered in Antwerp and elsewhere, should those hereby appealed to desire to help in the proposed manner.

There is very little time in which to make this appeal and collect and despatch any gifts, if immediate benefit is to be derived. Hence those merchants who may generously wish to support this plea (made to me by some of their own profession), in large or small quantities, are kindly requested to acquaint me by telegram or post, addressed only to G. Alexander, 51 Hans Mansions, London S.W., and to forward their gifts in kind immediately, addressed to the Manager, Belgian Relief, c/o Messrs Harrods Ltd, Trevor Square, London S.W. (who have most generously placed a warehouse and a receiver at my disposal), whence I shall personally acknowledge them, and have everything tabulated and arranged ready for immediate shipment. No kind givers need trouble themselves by making any preliminary inquiries of me as to the necessary kinds and quantities, for I can only say that too much of any sort of foodstuff cannot be sent, or too soon.

The following is what is chiefly wanted:
Flour (very much required)
Oats
Salt (very much required)
Jam
Hams
Condensed milk
Biscuits
Sugar
Chocolate
Arrowroot, and all kinds of farinaceous foods
All kinds of tinned meats

But any other similar gifts will be welcome.

Lalaing, Belgian Minister
Belgian Legation, 15 West Halkin Street, S.W.

———

CRICKETERS' APPEAL

'Members of a National Team'

SIR – We, the undersigned as cricketers, ask you to accord us the publicity which only your columns can give in order that we may make a direct appeal to the vast cricket-loving public on behalf of the Prince of Wales's Fund.

This fund, which has been called into being by His Royal Highness to meet the countless cases of misery and hardship which must inevitably follow on the heels of war, makes an instinctive and instantaneous appeal to the generosity of the public, and we, as cricketers, know that there is no public so sportsmanlike and so generous as the cricketing crowd.

As the Prince has truly said, 'This is a time when we all stand by one another.' All of us as a nation are members of a national team.

We have before us as we write the vision of many a fair English cricket ground packed with eager multitudes.

We have pleasant memories of seas of faces who in happier times have watched us play.

If only at this moment of trial we could gather in the sums which have been paid as gate money at cricket matches, those on whom the war has laid a desolating hand would benefit indeed. The wives and families of our soldiers and sailors would at least be secure from want.

It is this thought which has given arise to this particular appeal. We ask all those who have watched us play, and who have cheerfully paid their half-crowns, shillings and sixpences as gate money, to step forward and contribute over again their half-crowns, shillings and sixpences to the Prince's Fund out of gratitude for the enjoyment the cricket field has given them in the past.

Let everyone who has followed cricket recall to mind the matches he has witnessed and enjoyed, and let each one contribute according to the pleasantness of his memories. Then we shall have for those whom the war has robbed, not only of happiness, but even of the means of livelihood, a truly royal sum.

Without any undue spirit of self-importance we may perhaps say that we have contributed not a little to the interest the public takes in cricket, and therefore we make this personal appeal from ourselves to all those who love the game to send whatever they can spare to HRH the Prince of Wales, Buckingham Palace, London S.W.

Yours faithfully,
J.W.H.T. Douglas
F.R. Foster
F.H. Gillingham
W.G. Grace
Harris
T. Hayward
G. Hirst
J.B. Hobbs
G.L. Jessop
W. Rhodes
R.H. Spooner
P.F. Warner
F.E. Woolley

4 September 1914

PHYSICAL TRAINING

A Vital Necessity

SIR – For some days past a friend of mine has been raging furiously because, while there is nothing that is nearer to his heart's desire than to serve his King and his country, at the present moment neither his King nor his country has any use for him. In the course of his raging he came in contact with a high military authority, to whom my friend, whose gift for rhetoric is by no means to be despised, unburdened himself pointedly and with considerable force.

The high military authority's answer was this: 'You are,' he said, 'a man of forty, and in very reasonably good condition for your age. You have plenty of pluck, you can shoot straight, and you would probably acquit yourself in the trenches quite as well as most Regulars, with a very little training. But, while you are reasonably sound in wind and limb, it is extremely improbable that you are in a condition to undergo the ardours of a campaign.

'It is as likely as not that forty-eight hours of it would knock you up, while it is practically a certainty that after a couple of nights out in the rain you would be down with pneumonia or bronchitis, or rheumatism, or a combination of all three. You would have to go into hospital, where you would take up valuable room, and the attention of doctors and nurses who are badly wanted elsewhere. In fact, you would be a great deal more trouble than you are worth.'

Of the truth of this there can surely be no question whatever. There are thousands of men, between thirty-five and sixty, who ask nothing better than to be allowed to take up arms, and who are constantly galled by such a spectacle as that which I saw today – viz., that of a couple of dozen able-bodied young men, who might be at the front, absorbed in the delightful and engrossing occupation of watching workmen asphalting three square yards of Victoria Street. Let those thousands take to heart the truth that they would be more trouble than they are worth, and that it is entirely their own fault.

An Exact Science

For there is no conceivable reason why this should be so, nor is there any conceivable reason why the recruiting authorities today should be obliged to reject so high a percentage – I believe that it amounts to about forty – of those who offer themselves. At a time when physical culture has been reduced to an exact science, and when systems have been evolved whereby it is perfectly easy to develop and to keep in condition every muscle in the human body, any man who is not long past the prime of life, or who does not suffer from organic disease, can keep himself perfectly fit with a minimum of trouble.

There can be few of us who have not, at one time or another, taken up some system of exercise, and have felt all the better for it. But the exercises became rather a nuisance, the twenty minutes devoted to them was reduced to ten, and the ten to five, till finally we dropped them altogether, always meaning, no doubt, to take them up again, but always too lazy to do so. For it is a curious thing that a man will take infinite care of the works of his motor car, but very little of the works of his body, though the former can be replaced and the latter cannot.

To put the matter in a nutshell, the majority of those who have been bitterly disappointed during the last few weeks at their inability actively to serve their country, whether they be young men or men of middle age, have only their own laziness to thank. As their memories grew longer they have allowed their wind to grow shorter, and their muscles flabbier, till the authorities have no choice but to say, 'It is very kind of you to offer your services, but you are no use to us.'

I am told by experts in these matters that there is no reason why a man of fifty, or even of fifty-five, should not keep himself quite fit enough to sustain even the ardours of the present campaign, and that, so far has physical culture advanced, a man who is now quite out of condition could develop the muscles that are used in marching without marching a yard, and those that carry a soldier's kit without tramping across the country with a dead weight of many pounds upon his back. It can, they say, all be done at home in a month or two.

The South African Lesson

I remember that, at the time of the South African war, many would-be recruits were refused by the authorities on account of some slight physical defect, such as insufficient chest expansion or a weakness of the heart. A good many hundreds of them went to the ingenious Mr Sandow, who, by taking a little trouble, added two or three inches to their chests or put their hearts right. Every man among them was ultimately accepted.

The lesson then taught ought never to have been forgotten, but it has been. It was that every man ought to keep himself in good condition in case he should be wanted. We have none of the inconveniences attached to compulsory service, and we are not compelled to tear ourselves away from our businesses for annual training.

As a thank offering for thus, surely the least that we can do is to keep ourselves fit. Had we done so in the past there would have been fewer heart burnings and fewer regrets on the part of those who have lately been rejected at the recruiting offices, while the accepted could probably have been got into trim in less time.

It is no use lamenting over the past, but, with an eye to what the dark and unknown future may bring us, surely the best motto that we can take is 'Get fit and keep fit.'

One Who Regrets He Hasn't

DISTRESS AMONGST ACTORS

SIR – On behalf of members of the theatrical profession, many of whom are sadly stricken by the war, I am appealing for money.

Sir Herbert Tree has already generously arranged to hand over to a committee of representative actors about to be formed funds accumulating from the performances – crowded, I am glad to say – of *Duke* at His Majesty's Theatre.

The money which I am collecting will be through the same channel employed entirely for the benefit of families dependent for a livelihood upon work in the legitimate theatre.

May I beg of you sufficient space in your valuable paper to call the attention of the public to my appeal for funds.

I need not remind those to whom I appeal that members of the theatrical profession have ever been to the fore in helping the world at large when in need.

Will generous readers of this appeal please send cheques or postal orders to me at the 'Era' office, 5 Tavistock Street, Strand, London W.C.

Yours,
Alfred Barnard, Hon. Treasurer, 'Era' War Distress Fund
5 Tavistock Street, Strand, W.C.

12 September 1914

FIELD GLASSES FOR TROOPS

Lord Roberts's Thanks

SIR – The result of my appeal to sportsmen who are unable to take the field to give the use of the race glasses, field glasses, or stalking glasses to our non-commissioned officers under orders for the front, has been most gratifying.

In the first three days after the issue of the appeal over 2,000 glasses were received. These glasses are being distributed as rapidly as possible among the non-commissioned officers destined for active service. I should like to take the opportunity of conveying their sincere gratitude to the owners who have given the use of their glasses.

Most of the glasses received have been of the best modern patterns, and it is easy to realise how valuable they will prove in the field. Those who do not possess field glasses and who desire to assist should send cheques to The Secretary, National Service League, 72 Victoria Street, London S.W. All glasses should also be sent to this address.

It will be my pleasure to send a personal letter of thanks to those who in this way contribute to the safety and welfare of our splendid soldiers.

Every effort will be made to restore the glasses at the conclusion of the war. In all cases an index number is stamped upon the glasses and a record of their disposal registered at the Offices of the National Service League.

Yours very truly,

Roberts, F.M.
Englemere, Ascot, Berks

———

30 September 1914

BOYCOTT OF GERMAN GOODS

Plea For United Action

SIR – I am very much in sympathy with your continued articles respecting the boycotting of German manufactures, but agree with you that it is quite possible that traders will not persist in this unless there is a strong and united protest from the public, backed up by their resolve not to buy German goods.

I would suggest that a Non-German League should be started amongst the public, with a nominal subscription of 6d or 1s, mainly for the purpose of gathering a considerable number of names. These people would be asked to pledge themselves:

1. Not to buy German-made articles for, say, a period of years;
2. Not to buy any article whatever from a retailer whom they know to be stocking German goods.

That ought to be quite easy for people in large towns. I am quite sure that unless some united course of this kind is taken we shall get back to the condition before the war, purely out of slackness, but if the wholesalers and retailers find that there is a big public resolve not to purchase at their establishments if they handle German goods, they will be very careful not to offend.

Believe me, yours faithfully,

G.W.W.
London W.C.

———

BRITISH-MADE TOYS

SIR – The innate mechanical inventiveness of the British expert workman has not had the encouragement it deserves and needs. Toy and fancy goods manufacturers are only working three or four days a week. Why? Where is the need for short time when orders for hundreds of thousands of pounds' worth of German toys will never be executed?

What are we to think of British toy manufacturers who have raised their prices ten per cent, since the war, and have even made the advance applicable to all orders secured before that time?

Let us get to business. The time has arrived when the German toy industry can be captured. But this will not be done if we look at the question from a philanthropic standpoint. It can be conclusively proved that it is possible to make toys more cheaply and more profitably in this country than on the Continent. With all due respect to the British manufacturer, the foreigner has beaten him in business acumen. He has adapted his commodity to the requirements of the public.

What is wanted is a toy factory run on up-to-date business lines, with a commercial intelligence department as a leading feature. Without the slightest doubt it would prove a sound, remunerative investment to the shareholders.

It means the establishment in this country of a new and flourishing industry with illimitable possibilities. It means the permanent employment of a large and an increasing number of British workpeople.

Yours truly,

B. Wilde
258 Droylsden Road, Newton Heath, Manchester

———

1 *October 1914*

GIFTS TO GERMAN PRISONERS

SIR – The letter of Lady Hulse in your issue of Monday is both well timed and badly needed. I have several times read of German prisoners in this country being treated as honoured guests, instead of the vicious monsters they have so often proved themselves to be.

Why is it that in this country there is always a class so saturated with maudlin and misplaced sentiment that it is always ready to bestow its pity and sympathies upon the wrongdoer? One has only to remember what took place in Belgium a few weeks ago, and, in fact, is still taking place, murder, fire and unbridled license by these modern Huns to see the monstrous absurdity of bestowing such acts of kindness as Lady Hulse refers to upon those of their number who have been so fortunate as to fall into our hands.

If these misguided Britishers have such a super abundance of charity and goodwill, let them spend it upon our own brave soldiers and sailors, and leave these prisoners to the care of the military authorities.

That they will be well looked after there is no doubt. We as a nation always treat our foes better than they deserve.

Your obedient servant,

V. Page
Gorleston-on-Sea

———

HOARDING OF GERMAN TOYS

SIR – Toys can be made by British labour better than they have ever been made in Germany, if only there was co-operation.

But I would ask you more particularly to make known the fact that several large stores and large retail toy shops, in London and elsewhere, have been buying up every stray scrap of German-made toys and fancy goods and are 'nursing' it ready for the Christmas trade in toys. Those goods will undoubtedly be passed on to the public as British, or at any rate, the goods of friendly nations, and this is just where the difficulty arises with those of us who are truly patriotic.

I remain, Sir, yours faithfully,

British Trader

———

2 *October 1914*

CHEAP SUGAR

SIR – In your excellent leading article in Monday's *Daily Telegraph* on 'Trade War with Germany', you mention 'sugar'. Of all the articles we import from Germany sugar is the least understood by the people, considering its universal necessity.

The point to note is, that Great Britain is the only country which does not produce sugar for her own requirements. For thirty years, we have, in a large measure, been dependent largely upon the Continental supply of beet sugar. From a small beginning a gigantic industry has been built up under the fostering care of the German Government, until the cane source of supply became severely crippled, as it was not able to compete in price with subsidised German sugar.

The Germans deliberately set out to capture this important market, and, incidentally, to ruin the West Indies and other cane-producing countries, by their cartels, bounties and rebates. It is quite obvious that individuals could not compete against a deliberate policy of a Government. Germany produced sugar for 'export'; that is her policy.

Since the Sugar Convention, however, many of her immoral trading methods have been stopped or mitigated, but she has, in the meantime, created this large sugar industry at the expense and ruin of others, and if she had not been stopped, even a little, by the Sugar Convention, she would have stamped out opposition and then charged us her own prices.

There are some (agricultural enthusiasts) who advocate growing beetroot ourselves, but at the best this policy would be one of a slow and doubtful growth unless our Government subsidised it for years, and subsidising any industry should be a last resort, and avoided if possible.

There are two methods of ensuring a plentiful supply of sugar on a safe permanent basis: (1) Encourage the growth of cane sugar; (2) keep the refining industry in our own hands at home. We have had practical experiences of the necessity for this during the last few weeks. It is not too much to say that if it had not been for the British refiners, sugar would have been unobtainable.

Raw cane sugar, and plenty of it, with refiners to refine it and confectioners to use it – that is a sound British policy, and this can be obtained by admitting raw sugar free of duty.

Yours faithfully,
Geo. Nightingale
33 Queen's Avenue, Muswell Hill, N.

————

GERMANY'S TRADE ENERGY

SIR – I was exceedingly pleased to read your excellent leading article in today's issue, as it emphasises the fact that the capture of German trade at the present moment is perfectly useless unless it is accomplished by such a reformation in our trading methods as will enable us to retain it when Germany is again in a position to compete with us.

During my stay in various parts of the world while in the Navy I have been able to make inquiries on the subject, with the result that in most cases the Germans appeared to be making headway, particularly in the Far East. This is undoubtedly due to the greater energy, knowledge of the requirements of the country, and willingness to oblige of the German firms. I am almost inclined to consider the latter quality as of the greatest importance, for German firms were willing to take any trouble to procure whatever their customers required.

There is another point which also affects the question, and that is the unfortunate idea which most young Britishers who go abroad appear to acquire – that they are entitled to at least as much time for amusement as for work. I should like to point out that this is not the way the young Germans look at it, and that this may in some degree affect the success of the firms to which they belong.

Yours truly,
R.N., Retired
Hay, Hereford

———

3 October 1914

TOMMY'S SONGS

SIR – Mr J.M. Glover is quite right. Tommy certainly ought to have a repertoire of his own. Then are many collections of soldiers' songs published, but the majority of the lyrics are far above Tommy's head and have no attraction for him as a soldier at all. They are mostly of the objective order and relate to his achievements in the field, and are absolutely devoid of the real sentiments that appeal to Tommy personally as a man, to his human nature and his affections.

The songs I refer to are mostly written about him for others to sing. The intimate note is almost invariably missing. He still marches to 'The Girl I Left Behind Me' and the 'British Grenadiers', but I doubt if he ever sings either of them. By my desk as I write I have many volumes that contain thousands of songs of the soldier – *The Universal Songster* alone includes 3,000 military songs – but very few were designed for the soldier himself. I remember when 'The Captain With his Whisker Took a Sly Glance at Me' was a great favourite with the private at home and abroad – my father was in the Army – and later, though not a soldier's song, 'In the Strand'. Tommy wants tune and a good swinging chorus, and the theatres and the music halls frequently suit his requirements.

'Tommy Atkins' misses the point – a soldier can hardly sing about himself – and the same argument applies to nearly all the new songs that are just now flooding the music halls and the market. That is why 'It's a Long Way to Tipperary' is so popular. The words of the chorus alone strike home to Tommy's instincts. In Tipperary lives 'the sweetest girl I know'.

There you have it in a nutshell. Where would Tommy be without his sweetheart? Mr Glover may be interested to know that there is more than one song about his early home – 'Were You Ever in Sweet Tipperary?'

S.J. Adair Fitzgerald
London N.

BRITISH WAR PRISONERS

SIR – On my way back from Petrograd I met Prince Peter Lieven at Stockholm. He had just been released from a camp of prisoners of war in Germany, and informed me that the British prisoners were exceptionally harshly treated.

Among the prisoners were about 200 Gordon Highlanders, who were constantly subjected to insult on the part of the guards on account of their kilts.

This continued until finally one Highlander demanded an interview with the officer commanding the camp, to whom he spoke as follows: 'My uniform is 1,000 years old, and has been worn by kings. If it be insulted again I will not be answerable for the consequences nor what happens to me.'

The Highlanders were not molested after that. Prince Lieven told me that the British were always served last at meals, and if there were not sufficient to go round they had simply to do without food. The parole of officers was not accepted.

I am, Sir, yours truly,
F.V.T.
London

P.S. Among the prisoners was the colonel of the King's Own Scottish Borderers, and a major of the Royal Irish.

———

5 October 1914

TRAINING OF BOYS

Value of Cadet Corps

SIR – At this particular time, when the manhood of the nation is rallying to the colours, it is surely a golden opportunity to give to the youth of the country the elements of a military or semi-military instruction.

Territorial cadets have not received much encouragement in the past, or we should have at our disposal now many thousands of young fellows on the verge of manhood ready and willing within the next year or two to take their place in the ranks of the Army. Indeed, some of the senior cadet corps, such as the Royal Fusiliers and King's Royal Rifle Corps, have each sent two or three companies to Territorial units. Their places were at once filled up, and now most of the cadet corps are up to their full establishment. As, however, their maintenance is mostly provided by private benevolence, it is a severe strain on commanding officers, who naturally find great difficulty in providing funds at this particular time.

A large body of opinion considers that service in cadet corps, boys' brigades, and so forth should be made a compulsory phase of education, and that a boy should be compelled while at, or after leaving, school to join one or other. He could take his choice – naval, military or non-military. There are organisations for each.

The question is the more pressing at this moment, as a large number of youths have been thrown out of employment, and are wandering about the streets, where they have full opportunity of getting into mischief, and joining the 'ne'er-do-well' class.

There are, therefore, military, economic and educational considerations which might well be dealt with at the present time if the Board of Education and the War Office could be induced to evolve a scheme to deal systematically and on a national basis with this phase of the training of boyhood.

I am, Sir, faithfully yours,

W. Campbell Hyslop
Junior United Service Club

———

6 *October 1914*

'MADE IN ENGLAND'

SIR – I am one of those who think that we made no inconsiderable present to the enemy when, under the Merchandise Marks Act, we stipulated that things coming into this country from Germany should bear the inscription 'Made in Germany'.

Let us now do a favour to ourselves by making it compulsory that at test all our manufactures shall in future bear the mark of the country of origin (not town or province) – thus, 'Made in England'. We may also then have 'Made in Scotland', or 'Made in Ireland'. And if our brave allies follow a similar rule we shall not, I am sure, object to buy things we want 'Made in France', 'Made in Russia', or 'Made in Belgium'.

After the war we ought to be able to rely upon the national sense of patriotism and loyalty to our friends to reject any and every thing marked 'Made in Germany' – a mark which, for good and sufficient reasons, we must hope the Germans will continue to use.

A 'hall-mark', as is suggested by your correspondents, which may be recognised by the few, is not so good as plain language, e.g., 'Made in England', or 'Made in Germany', which can be understood by the many.

Yours truly,

A. Tidman
Prudential Buildings, Hull

———

BOYCOTT OF GERMAN GOODS

SIR – In connection with the campaign against German and Austrian goods, I should like to draw attention to the case of season businesses like our own, which, owing to the failure of the visiting season, are left with large stocks of foreign goods sold only to visitors.

We buy for the most part through English agents in November to January, season accounts. We are already feeling pressed for payment. We have rent, rates and taxes to pay, and to live through winter and spring. In Yarmouth we are faced with the probable failure of the herring fishery, which generally brings a large sum of money to the town.

We are, of course, unable to realise any of our assets. What, therefore, are we to do if these goods are boycotted? We have been quite unable to obtain English goods of the same class.

Yours truly

A Worried Season Trader
Great Yarmouth

———

FOREIGN BANDS

SIR – May I, in connection with the campaign which the Board of Trade have organised for assisting British traders to secure trade formerly in the hands of Germany, Austria and Hungary, make an appeal to the loaders of society not to engage German, Austrian or Hungarian bands, as has been the fashion to do for so many years? It is a well-known fact that for the past twenty years organisers of British bands have had an extremely hard time, owing to the vast amount of foreign bands performing in this country. The proprietors of those bands have amassed large fortunes, probably every penny of which has been invested in their own country. This I feel is largely due to the apathy of the British public and society leaders in engaging these bands for their receptions, balls, &c., believing them to be far superior to our English bands.

I remain, yours sincerely,

Corelli Windeatt
Kingston-on-Thames

———

MUSICIANS AT THE FRONT

SIR – I am asked to compile a roll of professional musicians, composers, singers and instrumentalists now serving, as either officers or men, in any of the forces of the Crown. The particulars I require are name, rank and regiment. The roll will not contain the names of bandmasters and bandsmen in the British Army. I will acknowledge each communication if a stamped addressed envelope is enclosed.

Yours, &c.,

(Pte.) H.V. Jervis Read
A Company, Empire Battalion, 7th Royal Fusiliers,
Whyteleafe, Surrey

SCHOOLBOYS AND THE WAR

SIR – At the present time schoolboys all over the country are asking themselves the question, What can I do to help in the war crisis? Few except the senior boys can hope to do much during the present struggle. I should like briefly to point out to them in what way they can at present best fit themselves to do that service later.

I have taught in English schools for many years. I have also had several years' experience of Continental schools and universities, chiefly in France. My experience has certainly shown me a far greater keenness on the part of French, Swiss and German boys. The average Continental schoolboy regards school work as a business, which has to be done with a certain degree of efficiency; he understands that he is at school to learn, and to train himself for the struggle of life, and he feels that ignorance and laziness are things to be ashamed of. In a word, there is less slackness in French and German schools than in the majority of ours.

Now, I put it as a logical proposition to English schoolboys that it is absurd to give two or three hours of their time each week to military drill and to learning habits of discipline, care and prompt obedience, if during the rest of the week they are slacking, idling and doing careless work in class. I suggest to them that what England wants in its young generations is keen, careful, competent men, capable of contending in all pursuits with the pushing German or the intelligent Frenchman. I tell them that their duty at the present time is to cast aside all slackness and to make efficiency their watchword.

Would it not be possible to organise an Efficiency League for our secondary and public schools? Accepted members might have the right to wear some distinctive mark, and just as Boy Scouts are pledged to render useful service and to do at least one helpful deed a day, so they might be pledged to do their duty as boys by fitting themselves to be capable men. A moral, manly movement of this kind would be of immense value to the country. Will not the headmasters of our schools help to start it?

Whetstone

---

7 *October 1914*

SOLDIERS' WIVES

Appeal for Hospitality

SIR – You kindly published a letter from me at the beginning of the war in which I suggested that people living in the country might be glad of the opportunity of showing sympathy with our soldiers and sailors by taking their wives and newly born babies for a period of convalescence after leaving the hospital.

I had a very gratifying response to my appeal, and numbers of mothers have, after the good rest, returned to their homes much more fitted to face the trying future. Moreover (and the value of this cannot be over-estimated), many women have for the first time been taught how to look after their infants properly.

These facts, and the many touching letters of gratitude which have reached me, embolden me to ask for more offers of hospitality. Now that the schools have reopened there must be many vacant rooms in country homes. I am in touch with many of the hospitals, and shall be only too pleased to make the preliminary arrangements.

Yours faithfully,

Muriel Foster
18 Hyde Park Terrace, W.

———

GENTLEMEN PRIVATES

SIR – Could not some relaxation be permitted in garrison towns during the war in respect to certain customs prevailing in normal times? I refer to Oxford and Cambridge men who have enlisted in the ranks under a deep sense of duty, risking practically everything to help their country at this time of need, yet, directly they get into the uniform of a private soldier certain clubs and hotels are closed against them in those towns. Why? Because they are wearing the King's uniform! They may be members of their Varsity and

London clubs, but that does not count where custom prevails! These men do not grumble at their unaccustomed surroundings and associations in which they are placed, but at being practically black-balled because they have responded to their country's call to arms! Is there any sense or justice in this?

Yours faithfully,

B.R.E.
Tunbridge Wells

————

9 October 1914

OUR SOLDIERS' WIDOWS

Need of Provision

SIR – Now that the Government has increased the separation allowances to such a figure that it will provide reasonable comforts for the wives and children of their breadwinners who have joined the colours, the next most important step should be for the State to make full and adequate provision for the widows and fatherless children of those of our heroes who have sacrificed their lives to protect the hearths and homes of all those who are left behind, and some of the children of whom will, we hope, become our future soldiers and sailors.

At the present moment all that this 'grateful' nation does is to grant the pittance of 5s per week to the widow and 1s 6d to each of the children. This means poverty.

The death-rolls of our splendid soldiers and sailors are arriving almost daily, and widows, who have lost the separation allowances, will either be compelled to try to drag along as best they can on this so-called 'pension', or obtain Poor Law relief as a permanency, or the homes must be broken up.

May I implore you to give me space for this letter, so that the great heart of England may be stirred – by a knowledge of the deficiency – to press that the widows and fatherless children of our brave men shall no longer be reliant upon charity, however ample it may be, but that permanent and satisfactory pensions shall be guaranteed to them without further loss of time, for the credit of England?

I am, Sir, yours, &c.,

Fredk. M. Gratton
Aspenden House, near Buntingford, Herts

———

10 October 1914

BOYCOTT OF GERMAN GOODS

SIR – I cannot help thinking that the suggestion to boycott German goods at the present time, if adopted, would be much more harmful than beneficial.

The stocks of German goods now held in this country by warehousemen and retailers were purchased and paid for long before this deplorable war commenced, or was ever thought of by the English trader. The goods belong now to our own countrymen, who are doing all they possibly can to assist, by subscribing to the various funds, and also helping to support the wives and families of thousands of employees fighting for their country.

Doubtless all of these traders would much rather deal in English-made goods in preference to foreign, and are just as earnest in wishing that this present great trouble may lead to a large increase in our home industries; many, to my knowledge, are also giving practical assistance by placing orders for supplies with English manufacturers for goods hitherto made in Germany. I would also point out that the trader in foreign goods here has hitherto had no option; he has not been able to purchase dolls, mechanical toys, and the hundred and one other articles he is required to supply, except from foreign sources.

There must be at least at the present time a million pounds sterling worth of German fancy goods and toys in the United

Kingdom, bought and paid for prior to the war. To attempt to boycott the sale of these goods would mean a most serious loss to our own countrymen only. No more German goods are likely to be imported for a very long time. Why not let the suggestion to boycott toys and fancy goods remain in abeyance until the termination of the war is in sight? The Germans will then be seeking business; boycott German goods then by all manner of means.

The difficulties of constructing suitable machinery and getting into the correct manufacturing groove will preclude English manufacturers turning out sufficient supplies for some little time to come. The German stocks will then have been got rid of, and the market open to receive home-made productions.

Yours faithfully,

Equity

———

MOTOR AMBULANCES

SIR – I feel sure if owners of motor cars realised the urgent need of motor ambulances to convey the wounded from the field of battle to the various hospitals there would be many more offers than have recently been made.

The fact that wounded men have succumbed to their injuries, and that transport by train is painfully slow owing to delays at sidings and other circumstances, should, I think, call for a special effort on the part of all who wish to relieve suffering.

I have recently had occasion personally to observe at Sézanne and other stations in France the misery of our soldiers in the trains. I have spoken to wounded men lying on the floor of vans, condemned to one painful position during many weary hours of jolting. Such trains take from ten to twenty hours to do a journey which by motor car would be done in two or three hours. Surely with our many relief funds and charities this should be the paramount charity to engage our attention.

Yours faithfully,

Nora Logan
170 Piccadilly, W.

———

DOCTORS AND THE WAR

SIR – I see that Major W.B. Fry, RAMC, who is well known to us in Woolwich, together with a number of other doctors, was taken prisoner by the Germans on 23 August.

Our Woolwich medical officer of health, Dr Sidney Davies, who was on holiday at the outbreak of the war, is still detained in Germany.

Should there not be at once a prompt exchange, or better still a prompt liberation of doctors, so that they may at once attend to their duties under the most favourable conditions?

Faithfully yours,

C.H. Grinling
17 Rectory Place, Woolwich, S.E.

————

13 October 1914

MUFFLERS FOR THE TROOPS

Lady French's Appeal

SIR – I have been requested by the authorities at the War Office to collect 250,000 mufflers as quickly as possible for the use of our troops at the front. I shall, therefore, be most grateful for contributions either in money or kind towards the fulfilment of this object.

The mufflers should be two and a half yards long by twelve inches wide, with no fringes (but other sizes would be accepted), and the colour of the wool should be khaki or grey.

Parcels containing mufflers, if sent by post, should be addressed to me at the Manor House, Waltham Cross, Herts, but, if sent by rail, should be forwarded to Enfield Station (GNR).

I am continuing to keep open my fund for the supply of socks and shirts, contributions to which should be sent to the depot at 54 Beauchamp Place, S.W. I would venture to request contributors to either scheme to be so kind as to mark their goods 'carriage paid', as in many instances railway charges have had to be paid twice over.

Might I add that I have now ninety women working for me, both at Messrs Harrods and also in a room kindly lent me by Messrs Tudor? These women would otherwise be out of work owing to the war, and I am naturally anxious to obtain sufficient funds to enable me to keep them employed throughout the winter.

Yours faithfully,

Eleonora French
The Manor House, Waltham Cross, Herts

POSTAGE ON SOLDIERS' LETTERS

SIR – At a time such as the present, when the people of Britain are amalgamating to make the lot of the soldiers on active service as pleasant as possible, I think it a crying shame that my wife should be charged 6d postage on such a paltry article as six envelopes and a similar number of sheets of notepaper. As everyone knows, the pay a soldier can allow his wife is small enough, without having it reduced by such exorbitant charges as these.

Hoping you will have the space to insert this in your valuable paper, and probably bring same to the notice of the Postmaster-General.

I am, Sir, yours faithfully,

Coldstreamer, on active service

———

15 October 1914

OUR APPEAL FOR THE BELGIAN PEOPLE

Hearty Support From All Quarters
Duke of Norfolk's Letter

SIR – May I be allowed to say how thankful I am that the *Daily Telegraph* has set on foot the Shilling Fund for the Belgian refugees?

England's loyalty to treaties and Belgium's heroic sacrifice and stubborn fight to uphold the same cause are two of the great inspiring facts which this war will pass on to history.

Your fund not only bears a practical testimony of sympathy to those who in this connection are most worthy of help, but it spreads broadcast the opportunity of proving that the obligation laid upon us is widely felt by all classes in our country.

I remain, your faithful servant,
Norfolk
Norfolk House, St James's Square, S.W.

THE DUCHESS OF SOMERSET

SIR – I feel it is a great honour and privilege to plead the cause of the brave Belgians who, under storm and stress of battle against a powerful and relentless foe, with their small army, by the wonderful stand they have made on behalf of King and country, have called forth the admiration of the civilised world. May I hope and trust that the fund your newspaper is raising as our debt of honour to the brave Belgians will meet with the success which it merits.

I do not doubt it. I feel assured that everyone, rich and poor alike, will welcome this opportunity of paying their small tribute, and I ask you to accept 100 shillings with my best wishes for your success.

Alas! nothing can restore to Belgium what she has lost in brave men and glorious monuments, but the tale of the courage and heroism of the King and his people will remain in the pages of history, and prove an example to generations yet unborn. Neither time nor circumstance can efface the memory of brave deeds, and already the Belgians have enlisted the sympathy of the whole world by the patience and courage with which they have borne their terrible misfortunes.

Yours faithfully,
Susan Somerset
35 Grosvenor Square, W.

———

NATIONAL CHARACTER

SIR – Our attention has been drawn to the appeal to the British public now being made in the columns of your newspaper for funds to alleviate the dreadful sufferings of the Belgian people.

As this fund has received the approbation not only of His Excellency the Belgian Minister, but also of Her Royal Highness the Duchess of Vendome, and of His Majesty King Albert himself, your appeal is based on such high authority that it partakes at once of a national character.

We therefore have much pleasure in sending you herewith our cheque for £250 (5,000s), and with hearty good wishes for the success of the Fund.

We are, dear Sir, yours faithfully,
Huntley & Palmers (Ltd)
Reading

———

OFFICER'S DAY'S PAY

SIR – I see in today's *Daily Telegraph* that you are starting a fund for the Belgians. I beg to enclose a cheque for £1 1s for the same. It is about a day's pay. If every officer in the Army did the same it would, in any case, be some recognition of what we think of the brave country that has suffered so much for us.

Yours faithfully,

A.H. Wrench, Major
The Barracks, Wrexham

———

20 October 1914

STOCKINGS FOR THE FLEET

SIR – Please allow me, through the medium of your valuable paper, to make a public acknowledgment of my gratitude for the magnificent answer to my appeal for orders to provide 'sea boot stockings' for our Grand Fleet. The result of the letter you kindly inserted is almost bewildering, and I hope to be able to forward at least 1,500 pairs as soon as the manufacturers of the particular yarn and needles can carry out my instructions. Many of the generous subscribers have sent anonymously; hence my wish to thank them through you; but I crave patience from all.

I am in touch with many centres of this industry and the boon of employment of needy knitters in fishing villages, &c., will be incalculable. Every order shall be most faithfully carried out, and not the least gratifying part of our endeavours is the expression of appreciation from the Fleet itself and the friends of our gallant defenders.

Faithfully yours,

Agnes S. Fitzherbert
Norbury, Kingswear, South Devon

———

29 October 1914

WAR AND ORGAN BUILDING

Famous Musicians' Appeal

SIR – In spite of the efforts to maintain 'business as usual', there prevails a natural inclination to economise in cases where the object of expense seems, at first sight, to be something of a luxury. We venture to point out the danger lest such economy may produce, as in some cases it has already begun to produce, a distress which it is the main desire of everybody to prevent.

It may not be widely known that in the art of organ building England stands second to no other nation. Our land is full of organs which, for beauty of tone and perfection of workmanship, are unrivalled; and this result is due to the skill of thousands of highly trained workers whose lifetime has been devoted to their task.

It is not difficult to see that, owing to the many and far-reaching calls now being made on us all, in many instances the purchase of a proposed new organ will be postponed till 'after the war'. Wherefore we beg to enter a plea that such postponement should not lightly be made, since the result of it will be, should the war be prolonged, that an art in which we are as a nation pre-eminent will deteriorate, or even be forced, when peace arrives, to start its long and arduous growth *de novo*.

On behalf of the Council of the Royal College of Organists:

(Signed)
Alexander C. Mackenzie, President
J. Frederick Bridge
George C. Martin
Walter Parratt, Vice-President
H.A. Harding, Hon. Secretary
The Royal College of Organists, Kensington Gore, London S.W.

2 November 1914

FIELD FORCE FUND

Scheme to be Revived

SIR – At the commencement of the South African War an organisation (under the auspices of a small committee) came into existence, and continued to the end, known as the Field Force Fund, for the purpose of collecting comforts and clothing for the soldiers at the front. This original committee has now been reformed, with the addition of Lady French, the Duchess of Portland, Lady Sclater, Lady Henderson, Lady Henry Bentinck, Lord Islington, Major-General Arbuthnot, Brigadier-General Long and Mr Ralph Upton.

In South Africa a system of separate parcels was adopted, each parcel containing comforts for one soldier. Each man received one shirt, sweater, jersey or cardigan, one pair of socks, one pair of mittens, one small bath towel, soap, handkerchiefs, a muffler, leather bootlaces, a toothbrush, toilet paper, ¼lb of chocolate, some stationery, an indelible pencil, a pipe, ¼lb of tobacco, cigarettes and safety matches.

During one year over 236,600 of these parcels were despatched and delivered. They were much appreciated by the men, and greatly contributed towards their health and comfort throughout the campaign. It is now proposed to revive this scheme for the Expeditionary Army in the field. In doing so the committee desires to impress on all existing organisations at present engaged in providing comforts for the troops that the proposed fund will in no way interfere with or embarrass the valuable assistance which they are rendering. The intention – based on South African experience – is rather to bring all existing effort to the most practical purpose by establishing a central bureau, to ensure co-ordination, and so avoid, on the one hand, the danger of gifts being duplicated to the same units in the field, and on the other to make sure that provision is made for every unit. To do this effectively requires the cordial co-operation of those engaged in providing particular articles, so that these can be combined in parcels as above described.

Another important consideration, and one which, the committee believes, will commend itself to everyone, is the question of punctual and certain transport of these parcels to the troops. In regard to this the committee is in a position to announce that the War Office has been good enough to give its support to the scheme, and will afford the necessary facilities for conveying consignments of these parcels to the troops in the field.

Mrs William Sclater, who so ably carried out the organisation of the Field Force Fund in South Africa, has again kindly consented to act as honorary secretary, and will most gratefully acknowledge any gifts of the above articles if sent to her, care of Lady Henry Bentinck, 53 Grosvenor Street, W. Any money contributions for the purchase of any of the above articles will be gladly received at the same address by Mr Ralph Upton, who has kindly undertaken the office of honorary treasurer.

Yours faithfully,

President: Eleonora French

Committee:
Winifred Portland
Mabel Airlie
Alice Bective
Olivia Bentinck
Cicely Bentinck
Edith Sclater
Nettie Henderson
H.T. Arbuthnot, Major-General
S.S. Long, Brigadier-General

Hon. Secretary: Charlotte Sclater
Hon. Treasurer: Ralph Upton
Islington

———

4 November 1914

ABSTINENCE DURING THE WAR

SIR – Without wishing it to appear that I am questioning the high motives of the Archbishop of Canterbury in his appeal for 'abstinence' during the war, it is unfortunate it should be represented that 'not for many years has intemperance been so prevalent as it is now'.

Even assuming there has been an increase of drunkenness among certain classes – and it is not improbable that the amount of insobriety has been greatly exaggerated – it is very undesirable to suggest that a large proportion of the public are so degenerate and neurotic that in their hour of trouble they must fly to strong drink to drown their cares.

With all deference I would suggest that this does not accurately represent the situation, and that the weight of testimony is that the country is bearing itself in this crisis with admirable courage and resolution.

I do not know whence his Grace gathers his information, but there are many big centres in which there has been a marked decrease in drunkenness since the beginning of the war.

I am, Sir, yours faithfully,

G. Read
98 Thurlow Park Road, Dulwich, S.E.

———

A FATHER'S LETTER

Service During War

SIR – I am governing director of very large works employing many hundred men. Over 250 of these are now serving. Of my three sons one is in the fighting line, and the other two go to the front this week. There are many thousand young fellows still in Derby and elsewhere, as may be seen by persons attending football matches, who ought to be serving, and it is sad to me, and doubtless many others, to feel that any day we may be advised of the death of a dear one, and to know that there are so many who ought to be made to serve, and who would enormously benefit physically and morally if they had military training.

May I entreat you to use your great influence to make military service compulsory during the war and for, say, six months afterwards?

This does not bind the country to compulsory service after that period.

Yours truly,

Francis Ley
Derby

---

5 November 1914

PLEA FOR BELGIAN DOGS

SIR – I have just read in the *Daily Telegraph* about those unhappy dogs on some Ostend fishing smacks at Lowestoft. Could it be possible, through the columns of your valuable journal, to suggest that the Government should exempt these poor dogs (belonging to the refugees) from quarantine?

It would, indeed, be a kind act on the part of the Government at this time.

Yours faithfully,

M. Tharp
Merchistoun Hail, Swindean, Hampshire

———

SIR – It is with greatest regret that I note in today's issue of the *Daily Telegraph* a quotation from a letter stating that many Belgian dogs brought over by their owners, are taken from them and killed because the refugees have not the money to pay for their detention in quarantine. It is well known that the Belgians are very attached to their dogs, who labour with their owners in support of the family.

Surely the Government might supply free quarters for the dogs of these noble people who have done so much for us. I believe that Belgian dogs have drawn the light guns to the front.

Fair Play
Weymouth

———

6 November 1914

THE QUEEN'S THANKS

SIR – I am commanded by the Queen to express Her Majesty's grateful appreciation of the kind manner in which, through the columns of your journal, you have helped the appeal for the gift of belts and socks to the troops at the front from the Queen and the women of the Empire.

The Queen feels that the publicity afforded by the newspapers has materially assisted the generous public in so quickly bringing the Fund to a successful issue.

I am, yours faithfully,

Farquhar, Treasurer
Devonshire House, Piccadilly, W.

———

PRINCESS MARY'S GIFT

SIR – In response to the inquiries that have reached me as to the nature of the gift that is to be sent to our sailors and soldiers by the Princess Mary and the subscribers to her Fund, I have the pleasure of announcing that the gift will consist of a brass embossed tobacco box, a pipe, a tinder lighter, and cigarettes, and a special form of present for the Indian troops.

To make it possible for every sailor afloat and every soldier at the front to receive this token of admiration and affection at Christmas time, I venture to appeal to the public for further subscriptions.

All subscriptions should be sent to her Royal Highness Princess Mary, Buckingham Palace.

I am, Sir, your obedient servant,

Devonshire, Chairman of Committee
Ritz Hotel, Piccadilly, W.

———

11 November 1914

THE REAL SHIRKER

SIR – 'One of the Cowards' has chosen a very incorrect *nom de plume*. He is not of the too numerous class of shirkers, of whom we are all getting ashamed. He must be consoled by the fact that his real grit is acknowledged. I fear, however, that the country cannot put the screw on employers, and that he will have to be contented with service at home, such as can be done whilst he is remaining in his employment. Such service is of great national value.

We have in England and Wales 5,685,175 males between the ages of nineteen and thirty-eight. Many of them are doing indispensable work in factories, foundries, mines, &c. But what of the others, thousands of whom may have been seen in the City of London alone, and more than half of them unmarried?

The real shirker is the man of military age who has no one dependent on his earnings and who fails in the present emergency to recognise his very obvious duty to his country. If these shirkers have to be forced into the Army by compulsory measures they can never be on any equality with the true men who volunteer. The humiliation of their position will last all their lives, and the realisation of it will become more acute as they get older. War with all its misery has some compensations, not the least of which is that we get near the true perspective of things.

Yours, &c.,

An Old Soldier

---

1 December 1914

MR KEIR HARDIE

SIR – You gave prominence in your issue on Saturday to a paragraph stating that Mr Keir Hardie declares, 'I have never said or written anything to dissuade our young men from enlisting. I know too well all there is at stake.' I am glad to find that he has at last felt compelled to offer some explanation to his constituents and to organisations that he influences.

He neglected the many opportunities he had to explain before the House of Commons, the fairest jury in the world, why he wrote the wicked paragraphs I read to the House.

If he is sincere in the declaration reproduced in your paper, I invite him to withdraw the disloyal advice he gave to the Labour organisations. I take it from his present declaration, which I welcome, that he authorises me here and now through this letter to convey in his behalf the information to the same organisations that he misled them, and that he wishes them to use their influence to get men to fill in the form, stating that they are 'willing' to serve when wanted, because he realises 'too well all there is at stake'. I am sincerely desirous of stopping the bad effect of his writings, and of getting his influence with that of the loyal Labour leaders on the side of his own nation.

Will he also use his influence to discourage and condemn the silent underground, but steady and deadly intimidation of loyal leaders of workmen in many localities, which is preventing them from taking the open and enthusiastic part in recruiting meetings and effects which they are personally anxious to do?

I am, yours, &c.,

Edgar R. Jones
House of Commons

A JEWISH BATTALION

SIR – Will you allow me to bring to the notice of your Jewish readers the proposal for the formation of a Jewish Battalion?

From personal inquiries made and information given to me there is good reason to believe that the formation of a Jewish unit for active service would meet the wishes of a considerable number of Jews who are not willing, at all events not eager, to enlist under other conditions. Such a corps might also be able to enrol Jews who are still subjects of Britain's Allies.

The formation of this unit must in no wise be regarded a movement against the enlistment of Jews in other regiments. But the War Office has already recognised that many persons prefer to serve with 'their pals'; to those Jews who feel this rather keenly the Jewish unit will be an additional recruiting measure.

Everything that will give this country more men without extra trouble must surely be welcome to most Jews in this country who, like myself, have just now one chief aim – to give all possible help to England. At such a moment we Jews can at least follow the lead of the politicians – sink all our differences and unite in this common purpose.

If, as I have every reason to expect, there is sufficient response, a private meeting will be called on an evening at an early date, so that immediate steps may be taken towards active recruiting by means of public meetings in the Jewish centres of population, and by such other means as may be desirable.

Let me repeat, this is not a movement of opposition towards other Jewish ideals or other Jews; it is a practical step to get soldiers who would not be obtainable by other means, and good soldiers too, as I know.

Will those interested communicate with me immediately?

Yours, &c.,

M.D. Eden
7 Welbeck Street, W.

———

THE FOOTBALLERS' CHANCE

SIR – Without entering into the controversy as to whether football should cease or not, may I point out that there is an honourable alternative for the man who ought to serve his country and yet must play and talk football – namely, to join the 2nd Sportsman's Battalion Royal Fusiliers, the battalion which is now recruiting at this hotel.

The corps already contains well-known footballers, and friends joining at the same time, who have interests in common, can be kept together, live in the same hut, and so on. They need not altogether sacrifice their love of sport while training for the great international now being played in northern France.

Provided the applicant is a gentleman and thoroughly fit, expense need not stand in his way, for he is not asked to pay for anything. The age limit, specially extended in this case by the War Office to 45, will attract many who are willing to serve, but unable to enter any other corps.

The battalion is an infantry one, and, of course, part of the Regular Army.

I am, yours faithfully,

E. Cunliffe Owen, Chief Recruiting Officer
Hotel Cecil, Strand, W.C.

———

2 December 1914

OUR SOLDIERS AND SAILORS

Presents for the Children

SIR – Will you be good enough to allow us to make an appeal to the readers of your paper for dolls, toys, books and games for the children of our sailors and soldiers? Whatever presents are received will be divided equally between the children of the two services.

Parcels or gifts of money for this object will be gratefully acknowledged, and should be sent on or before 19 December to Mrs Tillyer Tatham, Kendall Hall, Elstree, Herts, or Miss Meadows Taylor, Colney Park, St Albans.

Parcels, if sent by rail, to Mrs Tillyer Tatham, Radlett Station, Midland Railway.

Will anyone help us? He who gives quickly gives twice.

Yours truly,

Alice Cornelia Tatham
Kendall Hall, Elstree

————

3 December 1914

BELGIAN REFUGEES

20,000 More Expected
Urgent Need of Help

SIR – We have been advised by the Government to expect the arrival in the course of the next two months of some 2,000 Belgian refugees in each week from Holland, until, perhaps, as many as 20,000 have arrived.

We have at present available accommodation for about 10,000 in family groups, and obviously we shall require in a few weeks many more offers of hospitality. Counties on the east coast, and to a large extent on the south and west coasts, having been declared prohibited areas, many offers have had to be cancelled. Our main necessities now are fourfold.

1. Accommodation for families of three or more.
2. Furnished houses or flats, more particularly in London or its immediate neighbourhood, are urgently required at once. There is an increasing number of refugees who hitherto have been able to pay their way, and could still do so if suitable houses or rooms can be offered to them without charge.
3. We have very few offers to take single refugee men. Yet we have on our hands a large number of professional men, doctors, lawyers, engineers, accountants, businessmen, &c., for whom we are doing our best to provide accommodation.
4. Money contributions will be gratefully received. Our total subscriptions up to date amount to £42,600. We have spent roughly about half this amount. Through our organisation we have provided for some 60,000 refugees. The business requires a large staff, and though we have many excellent volunteers who have given us their whole time for three months, many paid members are essential for the transport, interpreting, registration, escort, and clerical work. The charges for providing hospital treatment are always increasing.

The Government provides accommodation, necessarily rough, for reception on arrival. Yet there are a number of persons who, because of health or status, cannot be sent to the depots. We have to find temporary accommodation for them in our own hostels or in hotels.

And we are charged with the responsibility for allocating all refugees to offered hospitality.

The stress of the war is certain to continue at best for some months, and we are, therefore, bound to husband our slender resources for the purposes of essential organisation. We find ourselves obliged, therefore, to ask for further financial support from our countrymen, who are free from the terrors and ruin which accompany German invasion for the sake of our Belgian friends who have had to fly from their devastated country. The nation has undertaken to give them hospitality, and it should be not only adequate but generous, sympathetic and ample.

The title of our committee is 'The War Refugees Committee', and cheques intended for our work should be made payable to Lord Gladstone, the treasurer, at General Buildings, Aldwych. Offers of hospitality should be made to the secretary.

I am, Sir, yours faithfully,

Hugh Cecil
War Refugees Committee, General Buildings, Aldwych,
London W.C.

15 December 1914

GERMAN PRISONERS' CONCERT

SIR – The citizens of Shrewsbury are to be insulted next Thursday, 17 December, by invitations to a concert given by the interned German prisoners of war to provide themselves with 'comforts'. Can nothing be done to stop this revolting exhibition?

Surely Lord Kitchener cannot approve of such entertainments or of this method of trading with the enemy?

Is Belgium already forgotten, and the bestial brutality of her oppressors so lightly forgiven?

Yours, &c.,

Civis Britt

———

24 December 1914

GIFTS FOR FIGHTING MEN

Princess Mary's Fund

SIR – The object of the fund raised under the auspices of the Princess Mary was to forward a Christmas present to all the sailors serving in the Grand Fleet, and to all the troops of the

Expeditionary Force. These presents have been packed and despatched, and, it is hoped, distributed to the sailors and soldiers on Christmas Day.

They consist of an embossed brass box, pipe, tobacco, cigarettes, photograph and Christmas card. A brass box filled with chocolate has also been despatched to the nurses at the front.

The committee intended to include a tinder lighter in the distribution, but owing to unforeseen circumstances it was found impossible to obtain them in time, or in sufficient quantity, to despatch them for Christmas Day. It is hoped, however, in the New Year to make a further distribution, so that each sailor of the Grand Fleet and soldier of the Expeditionary Force may receive a tinder lighter or some other equivalent present.

The response to her Royal Highness's appeal has been so generous that the committee are enabled to place additional orders for a gift which will include a brass box, and as these are delivered they will be despatched to all his Majesty's sailors and soldiers serving abroad other than those mentioned above.

A further order has been given to provide a similar brass box as a gift from the Princess Mary's Christmas Fund to all his Majesty's troops serving the colours in the United Kingdom, and from information given to the committee they confidently hope that the above presents will be despatched during the next three months.

The Admiralty and the War Office have kindly undertaken to distribute the respective presents. Presents will be given to the wounded, to the widows or mothers of those who have fallen, and to prisoners of war on their return.

The committee have been compelled strictly to limit the distribution of the presents to those who are serving, of who have served, previous to and including Christmas Day.

Your obedient servant,

Devonshire
Ritz Hotel, Piccadilly, W.

ROAST BEEF OF OLD ENGLAND

From the King's Farm

SIR – I think it may interest many of your readers to learn that I, on behalf of a few London butchers and their friends, have this morning sent, with the approval of Lord Kitchener, two carcases of beef, weighing about 2,300 lb, for the Christmas dinner of those brave wounded soldiers in the base hospital at Boulogne who are able to partake of the true roast beef of Old England.

Both animals were bred and fed by His Majesty King George on his royal farms at Windsor, and were prizewinners at the recent Smithfield Club Show.

We believe it will gladden the heart of many an heroic sufferer to know he was thought of at home.

I am, Sir, yours obediently,

Wm. Haydon, L.C.C., Brixton Division
County Hall, Spring Gardens, London S.W.

———

ART AND CHARITY

SIR – An exhibition under the patronage of their Majesties the King and Queen, Her Majesty Queen Alexandra, and Her Royal Highness Princess Louise, Duchess of Argyll, is being arranged at the Royal Academy, which will open at the beginning of January and will take the place of our usual winter exhibition. It will consist of works of painting and sculpture, and in black and white by living artists of the British school. Our object is to form a fund raised from the sale of works exhibited, and the proceeds will be divided equally among the Red Cross and St John Ambulance Society, the Artists' General Benevolent Institution, and the artists whose works are sold. The latter is an essential feature of the exhibition, as artists will then be directly benefited to the third of the sum which they have priced their work. If the artist wishes to waive his claim to his share of the money thus accruing to the fund it will be divided equally between the two institutions above named.

With a view to making this exhibition as generally useful as possible, a committee was formed of the presidents of the principal artistic societies in London, together with five members of the council of the Royal Academy. Each of the presidents was asked to issue an invitation to the members of his society to contribute, and the response has been very complete, and something like 800 works are now being hung in the galleries by a sub-committee of the whole number, and the exhibition promises to be one of very general and varied interest. There will be undoubtedly much distress among artists during the coming year, and we hope for a very generous patronage from picture-buyers and the general public. It should be borne in mind that every artist who sells his picture is contributing at least two-thirds of its value to two most important and deserving organisations of charity and mercy.

Concurrently with the exhibition of British works of art, one or more of our galleries will be given up to the exhibition of works of Belgian painting and sculpture, the whole profits from which will be devoted for the relief of Belgian artists. The precise arrangement for the distribution of the proceeds of this exhibition are not yet settled, and the exhibition will probably open a week or ten days after our own, as there are difficulties in the way of obtaining the works from abroad which may cause some delay. Monsieur Paul Lambotte, Directeur des Beaux Arts at Brussels, has kindly undertaken to assist in the arrangement of the Belgian works.

I am, Sir, your obedient servant,
Edward J. Poynter
Royal Academy of Arts, London W.

27 December 1914

ON THE RIVIERA

SIR – It is felt here that much misunderstanding exists as to the state of affairs on the Riviera, and also as to the difficulties intending visitors may experience in their journey from England.

Those who may be hesitating about wintering in the delightful weather conditions offered by this climate will be glad to know (a) that the train service from Paris is almost normal, the journey only taking some four hours longer than it usually does; (b) travellers can book through from London with sleeping accommodation, *lits-salon* or *wagon-lits* and restaurant cars.

Things at Mentone are just as usual; food is good and abundant and everything necessary to comfort can be obtained. This beautiful place is as quiet and restful as anyone could wish for. Both the churches are open, the chaplains are here, as are the English doctors, and already there is a considerable colony of English in residence.

As all the men here and throughout France, between eighteen and forty-eight years old, are away with the great French army fighting with us the same battle for freedom, the assistance afforded to many of their families and the population generally by the presence on the Riviera of the habitual English visitors will this winter be especially welcome.

Yours truly,
D. Allison (Hon. Canon of Ripon)
British Chaplain of Christ Church, Mentone

28 December 1914

CHILDREN'S SELF-DENIAL

SIR – The children of this small rural school are very proud and happy to send brave King Albert a little Christmas offering. This small sum (5s 6d) represents some self-denial on the part of the donors. One little orphan lad, who was allowed a halfpenny weekly as pocket money, produced the precious coin with an evident pride and joy most touching.

With hearty congratulations on the splendid response to an appeal which has gone straight to every heart, I remain, dear Sir, yours faithfully,

(Mrs) Eliza Bradbury
Adderley School, Market Drayton

———

THE OATH OF ALLEGIANCE

SIR – A short time ago I pointed out the fact that an alien naturalised as a British subject is none the less a subject of the country of his origin unless he formally, and according to the law of his country, relinquishes his own nationality.

I might point out that a further inconsistency is that on being naturalised a British subject, the alien subscribes to an oath of allegiance that he will be 'Faithful and bear true allegiance to his Majesty King George V, his heirs and successors, according to law', and at the same time he still retains his allegiance to the sovereign of his own country.

No man can serve two masters, and it is obvious that his oath is, to say the least, a matter to which he would attach secondary importance.

Yours, etc.,

H.S.A. Foy
4 Walbrook, E.C.

---

29 December 1914

NATIONAL GUARD

City Guild Units

SIR – The admirable proposal of the Right Hon. the Lord Mayor to form a National Guard should meet with an enthusiastic response. Every man ought to know how to shoot straight, and submit himself to some form of efficient training, so that in the event of invasion he will have a fair chance to fight for his hearth and home. That he will fight is certain, but it is equally certain that every man found bearing arms, unless he belongs to an organised force, will run the risk of being hanged or shot off-hand, his family exterminated, and his home given to the flames. We can expect no mercy from a ruthless foe. What has happened in Belgium and France may be repeated here with even greater severity.

In view of imminent possibilities, not to say probabilities, every man who, by reason of age or circumstances over which he has no control, is unable to join our Regular forces, should without delay do something for his country, and in this connection it has occurred to me that the members of the Guild of Freemen, a body over 1,000 strong; every one of whom is a Freeman of the City of London (and of which I have the honour to be the Master for 1915), might usefully raise a unit, which could be enrolled in the City of London Corps of the National Guard.

Other associations could very well follow suit, and all together serve their King, their country, and their city.

I am Sir, yours, &c.,
H.S.A. Foy, Member of the Corporation of London
4 Walbrook, London E.C.

————

31 December 1914

FIGHTING MPs

SIR – I have read with pleasure Captain Spender Clay's tribute to our hero soldiers and his unbounded admiration of their heroic conduct in the field.

I should like to record my unbounded admiration of the gallant though modest captain. I know for a fact that he placed his estate at the disposal of the Army, offered his mansion for a hospital, found forty units for the Territorials amongst the workers on his estate, provides for their families' wants whilst the men are on active service, and has risked his own life in the fighting line for 'God, King and country'. Such patriotism deserves the unbounded admiration of his fellow countrymen; England owes its present sense of security to the sacrifices made by such modest heroes. It will be a bad day for the old country when such landlords are taxed out of existence.

Your obedient servant,

E. Courtenay Wells
53 London Road, Croydon

INDIAN SOLDIERS' FUND

SIR – My letter of the 12th inst., for the publication of which I am indebted to your courtesy, was only meant to invite attention to the direction in which the charitable public might usefully supplement Government efforts to provide acutely needed comforts for the King's Indian soldiers fighting in France. The response it has evoked is, however, so generous that I have gladly undertaken the duty of forwarding to various regiments the gifts that are being sent to me, and applying the money donations to the purchase of other necessaries for the same purpose. I take this opportunity of thanking all the kind donors for their generosity.

The public desirous of continuing their help to the Indian soldiers, and there is still much scope, may like to know what is now most wanted at the front, in addition to that provided by Government. An officer friend writes to say that 'Stockings without feet are specially needed by the men to wear under their putties, or they suffer badly from cold legs in the wet trenches.' And the medical officer, from whose letter I had quoted before, in acknowledging the gifts sent to him and answering inquiries as to further wants, suggests that (besides socks, Thermogene wool and Capsicum Vaseline, which we are already sending) the following articles would be most welcome: Chilliline and peroxide of hydrogen 'for dressing bad wounds which threaten tetanus or gas gangrene'; vests and pants; 'rough flannel coats which might be slipped on to wounded men instead of shirts, and roughly made loose flannel pyjamas, tying with a string à l'Indien; bed socks and pyjamas for the heavily wounded; felt slippers; and satchels, 18in by 12in, made of any coarse canvas with tapes for tying, for carrying the goods and chattels of the wounded men when they are transferred to the base. At present their boots, putties, turbans, &c., are bundled anyhow into the motor ambulances, and very few find their own things again.'

I propose with the money standing in my name to the credit of 'The Indian Troops' Comforts Account' at Messrs H.S. King & Co., 9 Pall Mall, S.W., so far as it will go, to procure some of these things. Knickerbocker stockings of which the feet are worn out would be very acceptable, but all socks and stockings should be washed before they are sent for despatch.

I am requested by 'The Indian Soldiers' Fund' to mention that their receiving depot at 29 Somerset Street, W. receives and despatches any gifts sent to them.

Yours faithfully,

Ameer Ali
2 Cadogan Place, S.W.

---

7 January 1915

COMPULSORY SERVICE

Would it be Welcomed?

SIR – Surely it is high time to stop the wretched farce of inviting young men to join the Army. It is is not to be expected that Mr Seymour Hicks's appeal, 'Your flesh and your blood are crying for help', will garner more recruits than the statement that 'Your King and country need you'; neither will 'pertinent' questions obtain them.

Under the sub-heading, 'A Fool's Paradise' in the descriptive account by 'Eye Witness' of the warfare in Flanders, as set forth in your columns today, we learn that the Germans still think England is decadent, apparently because we continue to rely on such a half-measure as voluntary service, while all other nations engaged in this titanic struggle are enrolling the whole of their manhood.

It is we who are living in a Fool's Paradise, wasting money upon printing and distributing invitations to householders to furnish the names of those who may be willing to serve – a totally inadequate measure only calculated to encourage the enemy to continue. There are many of us debarred by age and physical disabilities from serving who view with disgust, if not with alarm, the apathy (or is it fear?) of those who could compel the shirkers to come forward.

Men Who are Serving

I live in a little town near to some well-known camps, and have on several occasions had the honour and privilege of entertaining soldiers of the new Army to tea. Typical examples were two of yesterday. Men from Ayrshire, both with large families, who had cheerfully thrown up their occupations (one had sold off his pigs and other animals to lessen the work that would fall upon his wife) and come forward without hesitation to fight for the Empire.

They are now roughing it in a mud-swept camp here in the south of England, in a district where, to my knowledge, are many young men who, without claims upon them in any other way, are apparently afraid to risk their precious skins in defend of their hearths and homes.

I have conversed with many working men on this matter, and all are of one voice: that compulsory service for all men between the ages of nineteen and thirty-five during the period of the war is most desirable. They tell me of many who are waiting on the bank in a condition of half-fear to make the plunge, yet hoping to be pushed into the stream by sheer force.

'Shove Them In'

It is up to our Government to shove them in. It has been hinted that the farmers have not come forward well, but in the south-west of England, and probably elsewhere, there are villages from which the farmers have gone off to the fighting ranks with their sons, the labourers have followed their masters, and the women and lads are left to carry on the farm work as best they can.

On the other hand, in many districts, down south at least, there are dozens of young men, sons of shopkeepers, wealthy and otherwise, who could well be spared at this time of grave national peril.

Yours, &c.,

Patriot

P.S. The warning to slackers voiced by Dr Macnamara on Sunday encourages the hope that the Government will not allow them to evade their obvious duty.

OUR WOUNDED SOLDIERS

SIR – For some months I have been devoting my time to visiting our wounded heroes. It has brought home to note as nothing else could have done, without being on the spot, the cruel hardships and sufferings these men have gone through to save their country from the horrors and atrocities that have been perpetrated in Belgium. Their patience and cheerfulness under great suffering can hardly be described. Some of these poor fellows, alas! will be crippled for life. I have seen several cases where the sight of both eyes is lost. What has caused me more pain than anything else is the mental suffering these poor fellows endure. They do not know what is to become of them. I endeavoured to assure them that they need not worry, that a grateful country would see to it that they did not want; but they said they had been told that so often, only to be deceived, and I found it impossible to reassure them.

Now it is inconceivable to me that these men will not be amply provided for. The country would not suffer it. Would it not be possible for the War Office to give instructions to the officer in command at the various hospitals to tell these poor fellows that they need not worry; to tell them definitely what will be done for them as soon as they leave the hospital, and so save them from the mental torture which adds so much to their sufferings?

It seems to me that mere humanity demands this. It would at once remove a load of suffering that these brave fellows ought not to have to undergo. I commend this suggestion most earnestly to our great War Minister, whose sympathy for these gallant men is well known; and I earnestly trust that prompt steps may be taken in this direction.

I remain, obediently yours,

Frederick Milner
Hopetoun House, South Queensferry

***

8 January 1915

COMPULSORY SERVICE

'Waiting on the Bank'

SIR – Your correspondent 'Patriot' has rasped the skin off the greatest blister in the so-called 'voluntary' system of recruiting when he refers to 'the many who are waiting on the bank, in a condition of half-fear to make the plunge, yet hoping to be pushed into the stream by sheer force'.

That is the simple fact. Hundreds of thousands of young men fit for service are today held back by a variety of domestic or sentimental appeals who would breathe a tremendous sigh of relief if they were suddenly ticked off by a recruiting sergeant, and compelled to go without another moment in which to procrastinate.

As one not unacquainted with Germany, her soldiers and her fortresses, I may perhaps be permitted to suggest that by the time the war has been on five years Britain will probably have awakened to the fact that in January 1915, she should have been strenuously preparing the fittest five million of her sons for the front.

Yours very faithfully,

F. Annesley
Primrose Club, Park Place, St James's

AGRICULTURAL RESPONSE

SIR – The letter of your correspondent 'Patriot' in today's issue raises an important point. He refers to a statement that the agricultural community has not responded well to the call to arms. May I, as one who knows something of the agricultural position and favours universal service, draw attention to one or two aspects of the question which may have escaped the attention of the townsman, who is always ready to advise or censure the countryman?

I am in close touch with two agricultural districts in Surrey and Sussex. In the one, ten per cent of one parish have joined the colours. In the other, much nearer London, the sowing of wheat and harvesting of important root crops has been greatly hindered owing to the lack of labour caused by enlistment. If we look at the matter from the farmer's private point of view, is he likely to urge enlistment on the few remaining eligible men he employs? In some cases he has a young shepherd, and his flock of, say, 200 ewes is about to begin lambing. The heavy and continuous rains have thrown work behind, and when the weather clears there will be all the more to do. Perhaps there are fifty cows to be milked twice daily. A farm cannot be closed down or put on short time like a factory; and as a preliminary handicap the Government came down and took in some cases fifty per cent of the horses, without which the work cannot be done. The labourers know this as well as the farmer and have the sense to realise it. I know of several willing to go but unwilling to strand their employers.

Now, setting aside the farmer's point of view, the country is urged to grow as much wheat and other foodstuffs as possible during the coming summer, so as to minimise distress. I know for a fact that farmers are being prevented by lack of labour from increasing their winter wheat acreage. The Government have already given instructions that they do not wish for the enlistment of men who are engaged in the production of war material, as they are serving their country efficiently where they are. Surely the men who are engaged in producing foodstuffs of various kinds, as well as the important by-products of wool and leather, are also serving their country efficiently, and are already too few in number. It is possible for small farmers to leave their womenfolk to run the place during their absence, but for large acreages this cannot be done.

I have no direct interest to serve, but would only plead for consideration of the points put forward in measure of compulsory recruiting.

Yours faithfully,

Hodge

————

9 January 1915

OFFICERS' SPECIAL HOSPITAL

SIR – You kindly allowed me in November to appeal in your columns for £210,000 for the hospital for soldiers suffering from shock. May I report progress?

We have had a beautiful house – 10 Palace Green, Kensington – lent to us by the executors of the late Lord Rendel. We have adapted it to hold thirty-three patients in separate rooms, which, with the rest of the house, we have furnished. The house is quiet, 'detached', overlooking Kensington Palace with a small garden of its own. It could not be better.

We have collected over £7,700, and only want £2,300 more to carry it on for two years.

The War Office have asked us to restrict the hospital to officers, as they are providing a similar hospital for the men. This, of course, we have done, and the hospital is to be called

'The Special Hospital for Officers', as we are anxious not unnecessarily to emphasise to its inmates that they are suffering from shock or nervous breakdown.

It was opened yesterday, and the matron will be glad to show anyone over it who is interested in this work, especially if they feel like subscribing, even an armchair.

Yours faithfully,

Knutsford
Special Hospital for Officers, 10 Palace Green, Kensington, W.

---

13 January 1915

FIELD FORCE FUND

Appeal for Gifts by Queen Alexandra

SIR – The Field Force Fund, which has since its inception rendered such valuable assistance to numerous units of the Expeditionary Force at the front by sending out parcels of comforts (each parcel consisting of a shirt, jersey or cardigan, socks, muffler, mittens, pipe, cigarettes, chocolate, &c.) to the men, is a revival of the fund which carried out similar work with great success throughout the South African campaign, when upwards of 240,000 parcels in one year alone were despatched through its agency to the troops then in the field.

The aim of the fund is to provide these comforts especially to those regiments and units who have no special association of their own to look after their wants. Consignments of parcels are only sent in response to definite requests from commanding officers, so that any danger of overlapping and waste is avoided.

Where Help is Needed

Whilst numerous units in the force already at the front are being regularly and efficiently supplied by their own associations, there are, as experience has shown, many where the assistance of the Field Force Fund is in great demand and is much appreciated. Already over 10,000 parcels have been despatched and received, and the number of requisitions (over 37,000) in the hands of the Field Force Fund largely exceeds at the present time the material at the fund's disposal to meet them.

Experience has shown beyond doubt that the regular provision of parcels of carefully selected articles helps largely to mitigate the hardships and maintain the health of the troops at the front. Apart, therefore, from its humane aspect, it cannot be too widely realised of what immense importance this form of assistance is in advancing the effective prosecution of the war.

For the New Battalions

The Field Force Fund will continue to respond punctually to all requests in so far as it is able to do so with the money and material placed at its disposal by the public. In this connection it should specially be borne in mind at this juncture that the need of assistance will in the near future be multiplied and expanded when the new Army arrives at the front.

These new battalions, only recently raised in the present great emergency, will not have the same advantages that their comrades already in the field possess, in the shape of local associations and historic tradition. The Field Force Fund are desirous of helping them in so far as they are enabled to do so, but the measure of the fund's assistance must entirely depend upon the amount of sustained public support on which they may be able to rely.

Where to Send

Gifts to the Field Force Fund may be made in money or in kind. For the former, which should be sent to the treasurer, Mr R. Upton, at 24a Hill Street, Knightsbridge, S.W., the fund appeals to the whole public. For the latter, which should be sent to the hon. secretary, Mrs Sclater, also at 24a Hill Street, Knightsbridge, S.W., it appeals to all associations and individuals at present engaged in making any articles of comfort for the troops at the front.

The directors of Harrods Stores have generously placed at the disposal of the fund their warehouses and such of their staff as may be necessary to deal with all the articles sent.

The need is great, and so also is the opportunity. All, rich and poor alike, are asked to give what they can for those who are giving their lives for the Empire.

Alexandra
Marlborough House

15 January 1915

BANDS FOR THE TROOPS

SIR – I was much interested in reading your report of the meeting in connection with the proposal to provide bands for the troops, and I should be glad if you could mention in your columns that in Bournemouth a committee was formed, under the presidency of Miss Scott Murray, with the result that £400 has been subscribed, to supply all the regiments stationed in the district with drums, fifes and bugles. Also to another fund ladies and gentlemen have subscribed, to provide the engagement of one of the local bands to accompany the troops on marches out. For the latter purpose another £60 is still desired, as naturally the utility of the drums, fifes and bugles cannot be apparent until the men are able to practise on the instruments sufficiently.

I am sure I wish the proposals of the meeting every success.

Yours faithfully,

Dan Godfrey
Pavilion and Winter Gardens, Bournemouth

WADERS FOR THE ARMY

SIR – Would you allow me to suggest a suitable gift for our soldiers now in the trenches in Flanders, and standing for forty-eight hours at a time in mud and water up to their waists? Officers at the front have written to say that long fishing waders, similar to those worn by fishermen, would be most gratefully received, and would relieve the sufferings of our troops. Anyone having these waders to spare, or giving money to provide them, can either send the same to me here or forward the waders direct to the Expeditionary Force.

Yours faithfully,

W.S. Savile, Captain
Ven, Milborne Port, Somerset

———

18 January 1915

HELPING THE NEW ARMY

Proposed Battalion Funds

SIR – There are probably many of your readers of suitable position in a town or county who want to help the new Army in its efforts to get ready for the heavy task it will be faced with in a few months. Such persons of application can obtain full particulars of how battalion funds of considerable extent for the battalions of the two Surrey regiments have enabled their officers to supplement the appliances for training supplied by Government, with great advantage to themselves, during the month or so which has elapsed since they had the fund, and how a similar fund can be raised in other counties and towns.

These battalions are without any of the county or territorial associations, or local resources, possessed by the units of the Regular and Territorial Army, and are fulfilling their duty of training themselves in camps far removed from the possibility of any such associations, unless set on foot by residents in the districts concerned.

The space of a letter would be too limited to enable me to explain exactly how such funds have been raised, and what is being done with them, but if anybody wants to help the gallant officers and men who have shown such marked patriotism at this time of national crisis, I shall be very pleased to send them full particulars.

Since we started the idea in Surrey and raised battalion funds for six of its service battalions, with the help of parents of officers and others of influence in such widely separated parts of the county, as Sir Charles Walpole, at Chobham, Dr Longstaffe, at Putney Heath, and Lady Scott, at Guildford, marked advantage has, according to their officers' reports, followed in various items, e.g., bayonet fighting, shooting on the short range, inter-trench communications, and other military and athletic exercises, though money has not been spent on anything the Government is likely to find within a reasonable time. The idea has now spread into five other regimental districts, covering some thirty battalions.

Relations between the battalions and their districts where they were recruited have also commenced to be knitted and made closer, which will have results in ways it is not yet possible to foresee.

I remain, yours faithfully,

Philip B. Pilditch, J.P.
Bartropps, Weybridge, Surrey

---

19 January 1915

YMCA AND THE TROOPS

Huts and Motor Kitchens
A Princess's Appeal

SIR – The generosity of the British public has enabled the YMCA to make a substantial beginning in France with its beneficent work of establishing recreation centres for the British troops. As rapidly as circumstances permit, the huts are being erected in convenient spots at the base camps for the comfort and advantage of the men, whether from the United Kingdom, the Colonies or the Indian Empire, who have already shown the greatest appreciation of what has been accomplished in this direction.

The Auxiliary Committee, of which I am President, has been formed to co-operate in the general scheme of the YMCA at the front and to organise helpful work in the various departments. Already several representatives our committee are at the British camps in France, as voluntary helpers without cost to the association. They have undertaken useful work, one of the features being the dispensing of refreshments at points of disembarkation and entrainment. They are co-operating in the management of huts, institutes, &c., of which some twenty are now in operation in France.

A valuable extension of these activities is now being organised by means of motor kitchens and tea and coffee trolleys, which will supply hot refreshments to the men, and will, we believe, prove a great boon at various points where soldiers congregate. The first of these motor kitchens has most kindly been placed at my disposal by the members of the Carlton Club, for the purpose of assisting our soldiers in France.

For the objects above enumerated, as well as for carrying on and extending the social work of the base camps in France, I venture to appeal the public, who ever respond so generously to a real need, to help us to raise the funds necessary to carry on the work which is proving of such inestimable value to our soldiers.

Victoria, Princess of Schleswig-Holstein
23 Bruton Street, London W.

AFTER THE WAR

Questions of Employment

SIR – Remembering the difficulties which arose at the close or the Boer War, and the neglect, in the matter of employment, of which many of our brave ex-soldiers were then the subjects, I would ask your earnest attention to a proposal which has been submitted to the Royal Colonial Institute and other bodies interested in Imperial affairs, the object of which is to remove the anxiety of many who are now defending the Empire.

In that proposal I recommend that the question of the after-employment of these men should be regarded as an Imperial one, and that the Home Government, through, say, the Secretary of State for the Colonies, should consult the London representatives of the Dominions, in order to ascertain how far it may be possible for their respective Governments to co-operate with the home authorities in finding openings on the land and in their rural districts, for such of the men who may be unable to obtain suitable employment at home, and who may be desirous of availing themselves of the opportunities and facilities the Dominions can offer.

I would urge this point the more strongly in view of the fact that while, as we know, there was a great surplusage of efficient labour after the Boer War, after this war the surplusage is likely to be far greater, notwithstanding all the efforts that may be made by the Government, the various municipalities, and patriotic employers of labour, and much suffering will ensue unless we proceed now to prepare, in collaboration with the Dominions, to deal with the question on broad Imperial lines.

I hold the view, also, that were it known that the Imperial and Dominions' Governments were conferring together on the subject, it would be a welcome assurance to the men now serving and to their dependents, and would be a material encouragement to further recruiting.

Lord Grey, I may mention, and others are cordially in sympathy with the proposal, which I venture to think should command the support of all who are interested in the welfare of our men at the front, and who believe in the unity of the Empire.

I am, &c.,

E.T. Scammell
The Royal Colonial Institute

———

20 January 1915

SOLDIERS' GARMENTS

SIR – It has been brought to my notice that during the last few weeks many garments and comforts have been sent to the men of the Essex regiments now serving at the front.

I understand that in many cases many of the gifts have been wasted, as they cannot be stored or carried with the regiments. I am venturing, therefore, to suggest that our kind friends should concentrate their efforts by sending money to enable what is really required to be bought.

The Hon. Mrs Alwyne Greville, who is in charge of the Essex County Depot, 67 High Street, Chelmsford, would be glad to receive donations or comforts, and will try and forward from time to time those things which are wanted.

The requirements of the regiments will be notified to her by Colonel Wood, of the depot at Warley.

I trust that this plan meets with your approval, and that thereby great waste and overlapping will be avoided.

I am, &c.,
Warwick, Lord-Lieutenant County of Essex
Easton Lodge, Dunmow, Essex

———

19 March 1915

ENEMY ALIENS

Women's Protest

SIR – Will you allow me to call attention once more to the monster protest we, the women of Great Britain and Ireland, are sending to the House of Commons on the subject of the enemy aliens still living among us?

In no other country at war with another can such a thing be seen as enemies living along coasts and in the large towns quite at their ease, in many cases in great affluence. Nothing ought to be refused to the women of Great Britain on this subject. It is no more than a reasonable request that those enemies of military age should be interned and the pest removed from our coasts.

The Government have to thank the women of Great Britain for the glorious way our men have behaved at the front. Never once has there been an unchivalrous act recorded, either towards women and their foes, and here the influence of their womenkind has come in. The hand that rocks the cradle rules the world, and thank God the appalling deeds of the Germans can never be done by Englishmen.

Therefore I say honour their women and let the Government do as we ask.

Yours,

Edith Glanusk
30 Bruton Street, W.

———

23 April 1915

EMPLOYERS AND WAR

Patriotic Propaganda

SIR – In connection with their recruiting campaign amongst employers the National Patriotic Association asked for suggestions, and from the thousands of replies to hand a majority include the following ten recommendations. Coming from businessmen all over the country, it occurs to me that you may think them worthy of publication on St George's Day.

The period proposed to be devoted to making a serious endeavour to rouse the nation to a sense of the position is from tomorrow (St George's Day), until 24 June (St John's Day), with special celebrations on Empire Day (Whit Monday), and the proposals which appear to find general favour may be summarised as follows:

1. That a special appeal be made for voluntary total abstinence during those two months.
2. That Empire Day, which falls on Whit Monday, 24 May, shall be observed as a Red Cross Day everywhere.
3. That the newly authorised badge of the Red Cross and St John Societies shall be generally worn as a mark of sympathy and seriousness during all that time, but particularly on the three days mentioned. Over a quarter of a million of these badges were sold during the first three days after issue this week.

4. That in the interests of our workers, as well as our soldiers in training, all clocks and watches shall be put forward an hour on St George's Day, and so give 'daylight saving' two months' fair trial at a most opportune time.

5. That on one of the three days mentioned great processions shall go to Hyde Park and other places in the country, where solemn services shall be conducted from as many platforms as may be necessary.

6. That a genuine attempt be made to schedule and co-ordinate the numberless charitable and patriotic schemes which have been started, so as to get the best possible results with as little waste and overlapping as possible.

7. That during the two months in question every employer shall give an undertaking that when engaging new hands after the war preference shall always be given to those who have served their country under arms or making them. With the help of the *Daily Telegraph* this recommendation should be carried out splendidly.

8. That the future of all incapacitated soldiers and sailors shall he made absolutely secure before Midsummer.

9. That the Government should soon appoint a home and Colonial non-party business committee to consider the grave questions involved by the new conditions which will be created directly after the war under the headings of Employment, Industry and Commerce.

10. That all employers be compelled to guarantee reinstatement to men who leave present situations to join the colours or to assist in making munitions of war.

A personal appeal to employers drew 35,000 to the Army in two months last autumn, but the attitude of many

Government offices, banks, business houses, and factories today is detrimental to recruiting, and thousands of willing men are thus more or less 'shirkers by compulsion'.

Yours faithfully,

George Pragnell, Chairman Employers' Territorial Association
22 St Paul's Churchyard, E.C.

———

29 April 1915

BRITISH PRISONERS

A Suggestion

SIR – The recently issued White Paper of the Foreign Office has furnished an authoritative statement of the treatment accorded to English prisoners in Germany, and this grave matter was yesterday debated in both Houses of Parliament. In the *Daily Telegraph* you have published accounts which fully confirm our worst suspicions, and you have besides drawn repeated attention in your leading articles to a subject in the last degree discreditable to the Germans and humiliating to ourselves. If we tell the Germans that we are not so inhuman as they are, and that their kith and kin in our places of detention are treated with consideration and respect, they simply refuse to believe us. Even the report of American Consuls, who are clearly neutral in such matters, they look at with suspicion and mistrust, because they think that we employ means to hoodwink such authorities and only show them what we choose.

In circumstances like these I wish to suggest that an appeal should be made to the Germans in our midst, many of whom have attained to a high position in our land, and all of whom have received from us not only hospitality in the past, but a large measure of courtesy and consideration in the present. It was mentioned in the *Daily Telegraph* the other day that out of a total of over 27,000 male Germans above the age of seventeen in the United Kingdom, only 8,600 have been interned. Moreover, a considerable number have been released – up to 5 December last 600 had been liberated. On the other hand, practically all male British subjects in Germany are believed to be interned.

In view of so flagrant a contrast as this, I submit that it is incumbent on Germans living in England – and especially those who have become naturalised subjects – to make representations to the Berlin authorities on the real facts of the case. Let them make it clear in Germany that England treats her prisoners, not only with the ordinary consideration due to all human beings, but with a sense of chivalry besides. She gives them such measure of liberty as is possible, opportunities for refreshment and exercise, and a treatment which does not wound their self-respect. I would also ask the Germans in our midst to appeal to their Fatherland on behalf of captive Englishmen, so that they may be exempt from such humiliating barbarities as those which have shocked the conscience of the civilised world. Probably they, in virtue of their blood, will be listened to and believed, even though our own protests are passed by unheeded or stigmatised as fictions. I think it is a clear duty, a matter of distinct obligation, that Germans who owe their wealth, their position and their safety to free England should use their influence with their native country on behalf of their adopted country, and thus prove that in this crisis of their fate and of ours they recognise a debt of gratitude to the land which for so long they have made their home.

Faithfully yours,

Scrutator
London

---

1 May 1915

THE KAISER'S BANNER

British-American's Protest

SIR – Being a reader, both here and in the city of New York, USA, of your valuable paper, I beg to call your attention to one of the most disgraceful things of this present war.

On Wednesday, in company with friends, I visited Windsor Castle. Whilst there I went to St George's Chapel, and was indeed horrified, and naturally very indignant, with others, to find in the chapel, over the choir stalls, the banners of the German Emperor, the Emperor of Austria and the Crown Prince still hanging.

I feel bound, although an American citizen, as I have brothers at the front fighting against these barbarians and pirates, as your paper has justly termed them, to call your attention to this injustice to the English people and insult to the mothers, wives and families of those who are so courageously shedding their blood against these Huns.

I am, dear Sir, yours very obediently,

Wm. J. Gammon, British-American
Sunbury-on-Thames, Middlesex

––––

HOW MANY DRUNKARDS?

SIR – As a mere member of the public, I am anxious to be enlightened on a certain point in connection with the new liquor legislation announced on Thursday.

Changes are to be made which will be felt as oppressive by every person in these islands who makes even the most moderate regular use of beer, wine or spirits; which will profoundly disorganise every industry concerned, and gravely affect the revenue.

The sole reason put forward for the making of these changes is that some working men, in some districts, are drinking so much as to render them inefficient as armament or munition workers.

Will Mr Lloyd tell us, quite roughly – within a thousand or two, let us say – what is the number of these delinquents upon whose account this sweeping legislation is proposed?

When we know this, we shall be better able to judge whether the disease – which undoubtedly needs to be cured – is being treated with ordinary common sense.

I am, &c.,

Inquisitive

————

4 May 1915

THE TREATMENT OF WAR PRISONERS

A German's Tribute

SIR – With reference to the suggestion put forward in the *Daily Telegraph* by Scrutator regarding British prisoners, I shall be glad if you will have the courtesy to publish my own views. I consider Scrutator's suggestion – that Germans in England should state their views as to the treatment of their fellows in England – an excellent one. I also think that Scrutator's suggestion would have the desired effect. Unfortunately, there can be but little doubt that the German mind is so constituted as to render a discreditable treatment of helpless prisoners not only possible but probable and I think that an appeal from Germans in England and, above all, from German prisoners in England, to the German public would result in an amelioration of the conditions now prevailing in Germany.

I fully share Scrutator's opinion that it is an urgent duty of loyal Germans in this country to come forward and testify to the courtesy and consideration extended to them in the country of their adoption and choice by practically the whole of the British public, at a time and under circumstances most trying, and when even the most loyal German must bear without flinching the fact that his sentiments, however loyal to England, may be looked upon as doubtful by English people, unless intimately acquainted with him.

As a German by law I have been a prisoner myself, and I therefore speak from experience when I say that German prisoners in England are treated not only with humanity, but with sympathy, understanding and kindness. After my release I wrote, and caused a letter to be sent, to the influential *Cologne Gazette* stating all the true facts about concentration camps in this country, and pleading for equal treatment of British prisoners in Germany. As far as I am aware this letter was never published by the *Cologne Gazette*. I am afraid that such isolated and individual endeavours are useless, and I am of Scrutator's opinion that a concerted statement by Germans resident in this country and a concerted appeal by them to the German public would be more likely to have the desired effect, if anything can bring the guilty parties in Germany to realise the baseness and the repulsive nature of their actions. I am sure that loyal Germans in this country – the blessings of which they have learned to appreciate and to which they are attached in most cases with a sincerity and love far greater than they obtain credit for – would come forward in their thousands to sign an appeal to the German public such as suggested.

I also think that German soldiers captured on the battlefield and now prisoners in this country should be given an opportunity to sign the appeal, and they should be given to understand the reasons for such an appeal, for, being deprived of newspapers, they may not even know that their gallant erstwhile foes are being ill-treated in German camps.

The only question is as to the best means for bringing concerted action about, and perhaps Scrutator or some other personality of standing is in a position to set the scheme going.

I enclose my card, and am, Sir, yours faithfully,

British Subject in Spe
St Albans

SIR – Permit me, as a naturalised German (and British subject of thirty years' standing), very cordially to endorse the excellent suggestion recently made by 'Scrutator' in a letter to your valuable paper, to the effect that representations should be made to the Berlin authorities by naturalised Germans in this country, testifying to the excellent treatment accorded to German prisoners here, and petitioning reciprocal treatment for British prisoners in Germany.

I consider it the duty, not only of all naturalised Germans, but of every German who enjoys England's hospitality, to unite in such a petition.

I am quite sure that the German people realise neither the excellent way in which German prisoners are treated here, nor are they allowed to know the vileness of the treatment of British prisoners in Germany, because the German people are consistently misinformed by their rulers, the Prussian military caste.

Yours faithfully,

Paul Windmuller
72 Mark Lane, E.C.

————

SIR – Your correspondent signing himself 'Scrutator' suggests that an appeal should be made to the Germans in this country to make representations to the Berlin authorities on the real facts of the case, namely, the contrast in the treatment of Germans in England and British subjects in Germany. I am sure this suggestion will be heartily responded to.

I, for one, having lived in this country over thirty-three years, have learned to highly esteem the British character for its liberality and generosity. Having, unfortunately, neglected my naturalisation, I am legally classed as an 'alien enemy of this country', and as such have had to undergo registration, and have from time to time to report myself at the police station for the renewal of my travelling pass, which enables me to attend to my business. The courtesy and consideration shown to me and my wife by the officials of Brixton police station, as well as locally, is beyond praise, and contrasts most favourably with the treatment meted out to British subjects in Germany. Amongst my numerous English friends and relations in this country none have, since the beginning of this unfortunate war, shown me the slightest animosity (one single solitary case excepted).

Again, with regard to prisoners of war in concentration camps, I know as a fact that they are treated most liberally and kindly. If only the full facts were made known in Germany I am sure the German people would feel ashamed of the brutality practised by their military authorities upon their defenceless British civilian and military captives. I shall certainly do what I can to make the facts known abroad in neutral countries, as well as in Germany. I feel sure that the majority of the Germans living in England must feel very grateful to the British nation for the humane and generous treatment which is being accorded them during these trying times, and many of them will be glad and proud to become one day loyal British subjects.

Faithfully yours,
H.G.
Carshalton

REMEMBERED KINDNESS

SIR – For a long time I have been waiting to see if any German living in England would come forward to protest against the ill-treatment of Britishers in Germany, and I am glad to read Scrutator's letter, which invites Germans to do so.

As I have been in camp at Newbury and on board a transport at Portsmouth altogether for seven weeks, I am in a position to speak from experience, and I must say that we were well treated. There was never a case of ill treatment of any sort. The food was sufficient and of good quality, and so much bread at Newbury (five large loaves per day for ten men) that we were able to give daily to the young sturdy seamen, who, of course, can eat a good deal more than men who are used to a life in a city.

It is impossible to forget the kindness shown to all prisoners at Newbury by the commandant, Colonel Haines, and I shall always remember the day the first lot of prisoners left Newbury for Portsmouth. The men were singing 'Deutschland Über Alles' when Colonel Haines was watching them marching off, and a man standing near me said, 'Can you imagine a lot of British prisoners in Germany singing "Rule Britannia" in front of a German colonel?' My remark was, 'No; they very likely would all be shot.'

Where is there a country that gives everybody such liberty as England does? Where is the country that allows us to earn our living even in wartime, with the only restrictions that are absolutely necessary?

Let the world therefore know – and I hope it will reach Germany – that we are treated as human beings, and in accordance with British justice, and let Germany take an example and treat British prisoners, and especially gallant officers and soldiers, who have risked their lives for their country, the same way as Germans are treated here. Then, perhaps, we need not be ashamed of the country that once had a great name.

I am, dear Sir, yours truly,

Pro-British Alien

———

IS IT REASONABLE?

SIR – We must, of course, support the Government, who are supposed to be putting forth their best efforts to save us from the degradation that the *Kultur* of Germany means.

When the infernal German war was imposed on the European world, we, in common with all the other loyal inhabitants of the British Empire, flung our whole weight in to break the Prussian tyranny. We encouraged our sons to fight; we emptied our pockets to help the poor down-trodden Belgians; we drew on our reserves to provide comforts and necessities to our own troops; we suffered the loss of profitable trade with equanimity in the glorious cause; and we assisted our own friends who were punished (even more severely than we were) by the misfortunes of war.

The casualty lists brought to us the same horror as they brought to everybody. Our dead are lying in France, Belgium, Suez and in the seas. We do not complain. We are British, and we want the flag of freedom to fly in every land. Now we, who have been pursuing honourably and lawfully our vocation of supplying stimulants to those who want them – (we impose our wares on no one) – are asked to suffer ruin because a limited number abuse the goods that we sell. Is this reasonable? If it is, we must suffer in the great cause; but is it reasonable or necessary?

We do not contemplate without dismay turning adrift many reliable and trusted servants who are too old to take up new vocations.

Yours faithfully,

William Williamson, Managing Director, Haig & Haig (Ltd)

AN ILL-CONSIDERED SCHEME

SIR – This wild experiment in teetotal legislation, posing as an attempt to improve the output of munitions of war, will, if carried into law, most seriously affect our business and that of all other distillers. We shall have to reduce our expenditure in purchases of material of every sort, and in many other directions. In a word, we shall have to do very much less than we have hitherto done to keep the business of the country going.

We have no wish to shirk our share of the cost of the war in any shape or form, but we do not think it fair to make use of the present political truce to force on to the country an ill-considered scheme, which under ordinary circumstances would be strenuously opposed in every possible manner, both in Parliament and in the country.

Yours faithfully,

Dunville & Co. (Ltd)

---

7 *May 1915*

PUBLIC SCHOOLS BRIGADE

Reply to Criticisms

SIR – Our attention has been called to correspondence which has appealed in the Press with regard to the selection of members of the Public Schools Brigade for commissions in the Army, and, in view of the erroneous statements which have been made, we think that the true position of affairs should be made known.

In September last the War Office authorised the raising of a brigade to consist in all of 5,400 public school and university men.

Recruiting was energetically carried on, and we reached a total of very little short of that number. The need for officers for the new Army then began to make itself apparent, and, as was natural, in a brigade composed practically entirely of public school and university men, large numbers began to be taken from our ranks to receive commissions in other regiments.

This went on without any check until early in the year, when the brigadier-general and officers of the brigade said the men under them began to fear that the brigade had practically been turned into an Officers Training Corps, and approached our committee with a view to ascertaining the exact position.

We therefore made inquiries from those in authority at the War Office, and received assurances that the brigade was intended to continue to exist as a unit, and not as an Officers Training Corps.

Further, we were assured that there was no intention of drawing upon the brigade for more officers except in special cases of which there would only be a small number.

At that time 1,700 men had already been recommended for commissions. Since then further need for officers has arisen. We, realising this, agreed to more men being taken, and when this new demand on us has been satisfied a total of not less than 3,083 men will have been taken altogether out of our brigade.

We think it is only fair to the brigade itself to ourselves as a committee to make public these facts and figures, which speak for themselves, and surely afford a conclusive answer to the criticisms that have appeared to the effect that the brigadier-general and his officers, and we as a committee, have put obstacles in the way of men obtaining commissions.

All the men who are fit for and desirous of commissions have now been recommended for appointment.

Arthur Stanley, Chairman
Lurgan, Vice-Chairman
H.J. Boon
J.W. Orde
(Committee of the Public Schools Brigade, Royal Fusiliers)
Committee Room 65, 83 Pall Mall, S.W.

———

12 May 1915

HARD CASE OF THE WOUNDED SOLDIER

Insufficient Pensions
Sir F. Milner's Appeal

SIR – Is there no member of Parliament who will take up the case of our wounded heroes and insist on their receiving more generous treatment? I spent twenty years of hard labour in Parliament, but would gladly begin again if anybody will offer me a seat, so that I may devote myself to the cause of these splendid men. Since the opening of the war I have visited many thousands in our hospitals, and it has convinced me as nothing else could have done both as to their sufferings and their needs.

I have kept in touch with many of the more serious cases that I have visited, and I assert that the pensions that are being awarded to the men discharged as unfit for further service are not sufficient to keep life in them. On 23 November 1914, a paper was issued – Circular NRF, dealing with allowances and pensions authorised by His Majesty's Government in respect of seamen, marines and soldiers. In the case of the lowest grades, pensions amounting to 23s per week as a maximum were authorised, according to the discretion of the authorities, with proportionate increase for the higher grades. Your readers may be surprised to hear that authority has not yet been received by the Commissioners to award this increased rate, and the maximum rate which the Commissioners are authorised to grant to a man totally disabled is 17s 6d per week.

Maximum of 17s 6d

Already well over 2,000 men have been discharged as unfit for further service, not counting the thousands of men still in hospital. Many of these men to my knowledge were earning 45s per week at the time war broke out; many of them had formed comfortable little homes for themselves and their families. They have uncomplainingly gone through sufferings and hardships almost unparalleled in the history of warfare;

they have sacrificed what many of them value more than life itself; they have helped to save our hearths and homes from irreparable disaster, and a grateful country awards these pitifully maimed heroes a miserable pittance of 17s 6d a week as a maximum, and my experience has shown me that very few of them get as much as this.

I assert positively, from my own knowledge, that many of these men, just discharged from hospital, for whom plenty of good nourishing food is a necessity if they are ever to hope to regain even partial health, would have had to break up their homes and be deprived of what was absolutely necessary for them but for the timely assistance of the Soldiers' and Sailors' Help Society, which help cannot be indefinitely continued, unless greatly increased support is given by the public. I assert this state of things is a disgrace to the country. The Government pay members of Parliament £400 a year for attending the House of Commons as little as they please for a few months in the year; they are paying well-to-do people 25s a week per horse for keeping remounts for the cavalry; they pay 22s up to 25s per week per head for billeting their men; they are paying exorbitant rents for practically useless buildings; and 17s 6d a week is the highest allowance they will give to these splendid men who have gone through sufferings no pen could describe, and who have saved their country from horrors unspeakable.

It is indeed time somebody should speak out, and try to stir up the people to insist that justice shall be done to these heroes. It is true that the hospital arrangements are splendid. In all the hospitals I have visited I have never heard a complaint. The work done by the Red Cross is beyond all praise, but what is the use of patching up their poor maimed bodies if we are only going to leave them to starve?

The unfortunate thing is that so few people seem to realise the necessities of these gallant men. Millions of money are being poured out to help the Belgians, the Serbs, the Poles, the French wounded; even wounded horses are thought of; but little or nothing is being done for these splendid men. I write hundreds of letters every week imploring people to recognise the great needs of these poor maimed heroes, and to enable the Soldiers' and Sailors' Help Society to supplement the wretched pittances that are doled out to them, but I am told that they have already subscribed so much to all these other funds that they have nothing left for their own countrymen. May I suggest this, that for the first year, at any rate, the Government should allot greatly increased pensions to these men. With good nourishment and proper care many of them may regain some measure of health and be able to do light work.

Duty of the Public

Soldiers' and Sailors' Help Society hope, if the necessary funds are forthcoming, to add to their workshops in different parts of the country, where many of these poor chaps will be taught and employed at good wages. It is to be hoped that everybody will vie with each other in finding easy jobs for those who have lost an arm or a leg, and then the pensions can be revised, but for months after they have left the hospitals or homes, numbers of these men are utterly unfit for even the lightest work. The suffering they have gone through, and the consequent shock to the nervous system, is such that they must have plenty of nourishing food and be tenderly nursed back to health.

I am giving up my whole life to this work, and I have personal knowledge and experience of what I have written. I could fill columns of your paper with cases of individual suffering. I believe when once the British public realise the urgent necessity they will insist on generous treatment being promptly given to these heroic men who have given so much and suffered so much for King and country.

I remain, obediently yours,

Frederick Milner
11 Hereford Gardens, London W.

---

20 May 1915

SIR ERNEST CASSEL

Horror of German Methods

SIR – As many other British subjects of German extraction have given public expression to their feelings, silence might be misunderstood.

Nearly half a century of my life has been spent in England, and all my interests – family, business and social – are centred here. All my male relatives of military age are serving with the King's forces.

My unfailing loyalty and devotion to this country have never varied or been questioned, and, while affirming this, I desire also to express my deep sense of horror at the manner in which the war is being conducted by the German Government.

I am, Sir, your obedient servant,

E. Cassel
Brook House, Park Lane, London W.

———

1 June 1915

ROLL-CALL OF THE NATION

Large Employer's View

SIR – As one of the employers invited to attend the meeting of the wholesale and retail trades, convened by the Home Office, and designed to secure a further enlistment of men engaged in the distributing trades, may I ask your permission to suggest, as a businessman, that the necessity has now arisen for dealing with the recruiting question in a more drastic manner on business lines?

In fairness to the men of military age remaining in these businesses, and incidentally, in justice to the employer, we have reached a point, in my opinion, where the principle of compulsion must be recognised, thereby giving a complete system of national service.

Up to this point our voluntary system has achieved wonders. The Empire has not only surprised itself, but the whole world, by raising a volunteer Army of enormous strength. This splendid Army has been gathered from all quarters of the world where the flag flies, and trained by a master mind; and whatever shortcomings there may have been, inseparable from such a mighty effort made so spontaneously, it is still a triumph of organisation.

Business Firms and Registration

It is our pride that this firm has sent many hundreds of gallant fellows to this great Army. Several hundreds of military age remain in our employ, and, admittedly, there is a very large number of fine young men yet available in the great London shops – excellent businessmen, and therefore very proper men to be employed in a national service. But I am convinced that it is certainly not wise to take all these men away from their business usefulness until, and unless, they are wanted; and not altogether fair that they should go while many thousands of men throughout the country, equally fit, are not called upon at all.

For instance, under the system of voluntary registration now being pursued, my firm, with many others, will be asked to give a return of men of recruitable age. This we are pleased to do, and these men will then be directly approached by the authorities. Most probably all these men will feel the call to service imperative, and forthwith enlist, whilst thousands of other men, escaping registration for various reasons, will never be directly approached.

Untouched Resources

Now that the need has been shown for employing the best that the country can produce for national service in various ways outside purely military duties, voluntary enlistment is no longer to be relied upon. The latest figures give the total male strength of the nation, of conscriptable age, as seven million. On this basis it is obvious that vast numbers of men have not realised the necessity for their services either in a combative or an administrative sense. And the frankly haphazard method of our present system can never reach them, because it is not direct and personal.

Also, surely it is an economic blunder to use so many of our young married men (who are bringing up the coming generation – and paying for it!) while unmarried men, without responsibilities, are not serving. I think, too, we have to remind ourselves of the untouched resources we have in the educated young women of our country – the middle-class girl – who could be mobilised for very effective work in many of our national undertakings.

Organised Service

However effective voluntary enlistment has been for military purposes, it is clear, I think, that we now want a system of organised service, fair to everybody and helpful to employers

– a system which would utilise as it is required, and where it is required, the utmost strength of the country. From all businesses large and small, the Government would take just so many men as it immediately required, practising a scheme of gradual depletion until the total recruitable strength was absorbed.

At present many men of military age are open to the reproaches of others without deserving it. A national call to service would remove this. Men there may be (I have not met them) who do not wish to serve – these merit all our contempt. Coming in contact, as I do, with men of all ages, I make bold to say that our manhood as a whole is fervently patriotic, and, so far as I have gathered, is unanimous in the demand for the immediate adaption of a plan of a compulsory service.

It should be simple enough for a central authority, working through departments split up territorially, to compile a new Domesday Book, wherein every man, with the kind of service to be expected of him, should be recorded, ready to be called whenever he is wanted. Businessmen could prepare this roll-call of the nation very expeditiously – a matter of a few weeks. I am sure the system could be educed very easily, if the Government would lay it down as a principle.

Yours truly,

Sydney M. Skinner, Chairman John Barker & Co. (Ltd)
Kensington High Street, W.

5 July 1915

HELP IN THE HARVEST FIELD

SIR – There is one possible form of help which seems to have been overlooked.

For some years past farmers, or their wives, all over the country, have made a practice of taking holiday visitors. I have before me lists of over a thousand, which could probably be increased.

If some scheme could be promptly devised for bringing together farmers and holidaymakers willing to help on defined, if limited, lines, the farmer, on his part, might perhaps make some slight concession in his terms to such paying guests. In any case, if this form of help appeals to any considerable number I have no doubt a practical provisional committee could be formed at once to consider the preliminaries.

Apart from the healthy satisfaction of 'doing their bit', working holidaymakers would find compensation in the discovery of many new delightful spots in rural England.

Yours faithfully,

Percy Lindley
20 Fleet Street, E.C.

7 July 1915

WORKERS' SUPPORT

An Appeal to Employers

SIR – At this great national crisis, when it is the duty of all of us (including every employer who has any capital at command) to do our utmost to swell the new War Loan to really formidable proportions, we have felt it imperative to increase our holding of £100,000 up to £150,000.

Among small investors the easiest way to popularise the loan is to offer to pledge themselves to subscribe up to a certain amount, but at least £5. To do this a personal touch is necessary. An impersonal Post Office savings appeal will do something, but a reasoned appeal from an employer will do much more.

I think many employers may still be unaware that they can themselves use the Post Office department to hold any stock for which they pay and take up for distribution among their staff on payment (say) in weekly instalments. Out of £150,000 taken up by our firm, £140,000 for the company and £10,000 for the employees' savings-bank account, we have found it possible to earmark £40,000 to be held by the Post Office authorities at our disposal for distribution to those of our staff who elect to pay small or large weekly contributions up to an amount to be chosen by themselves.

To these smaller subscribers we will ourselves pay 5 per cent on their subscriptions until the amount of a £5 bond is reached, and after that will make the 4½ per cent interest allowed by the Government up to 5 per cent for a certain period.

As the time for subscribing is now limited to a few days; it is to be hoped that employers generally will make an effort worthy of the cause.

I am, Sir, yours faithfully,

Jesse Boot

————

15 July 1915

GAME AS NATIONAL FOOD

A Suggestion

SIR – Matters bearing upon public economy in wartime are now being discussed at length in the press. Much that is written, however, cannot usefully affect the situation, because its sponsors fail to offer remedies suitable for practical application. As concrete practice should take the place of abstract suggestion in these stressful times, it occurs to me to offer assistance towards insuring the more thorough administration of a most valuable food supply – the furred and feathered game of this country. This with troth, may be regarded, more than ever before, as a national asset of twofold value, for if this year a considerable portion of the game supply could be officially administered for distribution to the public, it would more than ever check the soaring prices of comestibles, and could to a greater extent be utilised as a welcome change of diet for our sick, wounded and convalescent soldiers and sailors, and all tending them.

Next month the game shooting season will be inaugurated by the killing of tens of thousands of grouse. Therefore the time remaining for the elaboration of methods is not over long. I suggest two courses for consideration.

First, I think it might be well if the Government itself were to supervise this important matter by actual purchase of a fixed percentage of all game killed, the provision of sufficient cold storage facilities at suitable centres, and means for the carriage of the game, and its most effective distribution. The railways being under state control, everything that would assist to insure the success of the measure is now in the hands of the Government. The prompt despatch of game from any wayside station to the local centre, without waiting for the collection of large consignments, might prevent wastage taking place in the hot weather generally experienced in the first haul of the shooting season.

Another method, alternative to the foregoing, would involve less responsibilities and a narrower scheme of operations. This plan might insure the purchase of a smaller percentage of game, its carriage and cold storage, for the use of our warriors, hale or sick, at home or abroad, ashore or afloat. Doubtless so soon as a proper working scheme were known to be established, many large game proprietors would feel inclined to offer and to place on rail, free of all cost, considerable quantities of game for distribution in this commendable direction.

I shall be very pleased to expand these ideas, and to assist the Government, or other responsible body, to operate any measures of the sort herein indicated.

Yours, &c.,

Henry Sharp
Sutton Coldfield, Warwickshire

———

VILLAGE SHIRKERS

SIR – It would be interesting to know upon what system recruiting is being carried out in the country districts in England. I live in a village in Bucks, which has apparently been overlooked by the recruiting agents.

There are two young men eligible for service working on the farm next door to me. A young chauffeur drives me from the neighbouring town to the village, a young butcher brings meat from the same town. These four cases have come under my own eyes; there are many others. I taxed one of these young men with not enlisting. His answer was: 'Plenty of Canadians and Australians; they like it. I haven't been sent for yet.'

As I belong to a family of which not a single male is left in civil occupation, I fail to see the justice of our system.

The last two of my own menfolk to go are a portrait-painter, over forty-five, whose work hung on the walls of the Royal Academy, and who is serving now as an orderly in a hospital; and a nephew, of nineteen, who, the only son of his parents, has come to England to enrol, being under the age limit in Australia.

Surely there is something radically wrong and unjust in the system which works like this. I enclose the name of the village, the neighbouring towns, and my own name in the hope that you can bring this district to the attention of the recruiting agents.

Yours truly,

Officer's Wife

---

19 July 1915

THE TRAINING OF MEDICAL WOMEN

National Work
An Urgent Call

SIR – The war has constituted a turning point in the position of medical women, and there are new openings and new opportunities for them in many directions.

Increasing numbers of women are desirous of entering the profession, and to provide for their adequate educational needs the London (Royal Free Hospital) School of Medicine for Women is now practically doubling its laboratory accommodation.

The council of the school has already received £15,000 of the £30,000 required for the additional buildings and their equipment. We would direct your attention to the effort started by a number of representative men and women to help to raise the balance of £15,000 by means of subscriptions of £1 each.

Yours faithfully,

H.H. Asquith
Curzon of Kedleston
Arthur James Balfour

———

20 July 1915

GOVERNMENT AND THE MINES

SIR – Coal being an absolute necessity for the prosecution of the war, and its production being interfered with by quarrels between capital and labour, the duty of the Government is plain. It should at once take over the mines and hold them for the war.

If this is done the question which is the root cause of the present strike, and which if allowed to fester will produce further trouble, would he settled. From profits a fair wage should be paid to men, and a fair interest on their capital to employers.

At the same time the consumer would get his coal at a fair price, while the men would know that their labour and the country's necessity were not being exploited by the employers for their own undue advantage.

Delays have dangerous ends.

Yours faithfully,

Robert Yerburgh
Barwhillanty, Parton, N.B.

————

23 July 1915

20,000 PIPES WANTED

SIR – I received a letter from Brigadier-General F. Koe, asking me to send out to the soldiers at the Dardanelles 20,000 wooden pipes, as if their own are lost or broken the men have no means of replacing them.

I should be very thankful for any subscription towards buying these, and will acknowledge the same. This number of pipes will only go a small way among the soldiers at present out there.

I am, yours truly,

B.F. Koe
Curragh Camp, Neragh, Co. Tipperary

————

24 July 1915

HOLIDAYS AT MARGATE

SIR – Will you very generously permit me the use of your valuable and most patriotic paper as a medium for an appeal to those about to take their holidays, and to say that the Corporation of Margate have made every provision for entertaining their visitors as in normal times?

I am sure it will be of interest to the public to know that definite arrangements have been made for the appearance of the following artists during the season: Miss Carrie Tubb, Miss Dorothy Webster, Miss Lucy Nuttall, Miss Daisy Kennedy, Mr Robert Radford, Mr Fraser Gauge, Moiseiwitsch, Mr Albert Chevalier and Ysaÿe.

Our magnificent sands – the happy hunting-ground for the children – are all open and absolutely as free as ever they have been, and the sea bathing, so popular on account of its safety, is also largely patronised. I am pleased to state that the many other places of entertainment, including the Jetty Pavilion, are all carrying on as usual. I sometimes hear it reported:

1. That the public are not allowed on the sands.
2. That we are under martial law.
3. That all promenades are closed at 6 p.m.
4. That everyone has to be indoors by nine, and all places of amusement closed.

One can only imagine that such statements (entirely false) are made in Germany and no doubt apply there, but certainly not in our own borough, now so well known, and which should be better known, for its wonderful recuperative effects on all those seeking renewed health, with all the well-organised entertainments of a high-class Continental pleasure resort.

Yours faithfully,

Wm. Booth Reeve, Mayor
Mayor's Parlour, Town Hall, Margate

STOPPAGE OF RACING

Effect on Horse Breeding

SIR – I see Mr Richard Ord, the well-known racing man, has written a letter in the *Sporting Chronicle*, making the interesting suggestion that a race meeting should be held in the north of England. Now, Sir, I yield to nobody in my anxiety about the war, and might mention that I have a son and many relations at the front, but I do ask why the amusement, if it is so, of racing should be stopped, though it carries with it the supreme test of thoroughbred horse breeding, while theatres and cinemas and concert rooms are allowed to remain open, which conduce to nothing but amusement.

The excuse we are given is that the horses and people cannot be conveyed to race meetings by train, and the only race meetings allowed are those at Newmarket. I am wondering whether the Government have realised that it would be quite possible, if the race committees at the various racing centres such as Stockton, Redcar, Doncaster, York and Newcastle wished it, to hold a race meeting without trains as Mr Ord suggests, and if this plan should not succeed, why should not one race meeting be arranged in the north, where nothing but north country horses might compete, and the same in the south, leaving Newmarket also as a racing centre? The horses have all been entered for their various engagements, and has it crossed the mind of Mr Runciman, &c., that all the men connected with racing, training and breeding establishments are now thrown out of work exactly in the same way as actors, theatre and cinema managers and officials would be should all the theatres, concert rooms and cinemas be closed?

There is another point on this question. Have they considered the depreciation the Government have brought about in thoroughbred stock? No doubt, people such as his Majesty the King, the Duke of Portland, Lord Rosebery and Messrs Joel can afford to keep their racing establishments in hopes that when the war is over racing may again be resumed; but take the case of the small breeder; take the case of the small owner. I mention two cases. The small breeder, perhaps, has two stallions, and perhaps ten or twelve mares of his own. Probably the stallions' fees for these mares pay for the keep of his mares and the stallions, but he looks for livelihood in the sale of his yearlings at either Newmarket July week or Doncaster. One glance at the newspaper at the prices of the last July sales will show in a moment that the depreciation is enormous at a time when every farthing that can be made will be required to pay for the war.

Unequal Treatment

Then take the case of the small owner. I have a case before me in point now of an ardent supporter of racing. He has two good yearling fillies. In ordinary times these fillies would be worth £500 to £1,000 each for their racing career, being half-sisters to good horses; but he has to lease his fillies without any bonus, the stallion fee alone being £300. He also has a two-year-old colt and a mare in training – not first-class, but they might have picked up small races; but, owing to the stoppage of racing, it is impossible for them to win a race at all, and such animals, unless extraordinarily well bred, just fetch the price of cat's meat. Consequently, he will either have to sell them for £25 or £30 – their proper value being £500 each – or give them away.

These are not imaginary cases, but two for which I could give you chapter and verse. The net result is that horse breeders and horse owners are to be ruined while theatre and cinema managers and officials are allowed to make profit. It does seem to me straining at a gnat and swallowing a camel to put an end to racing all over the country (though I base my main argument on the damage to thoroughbred horse breeding and the damage to small breeders and owners), and then to allow every theatre in every place to be crowded night after night when they have nothing to recommend them but absolute amusement.

This attacking of one industry and allowing another is part and parcel of the Government's action in wishing to fix the price of coal at the pit mouth, entirely forgetting the enormous risks and expense of sinking a coal mine, and then allowing butchers, fishmongers and nurserymen to charge exactly what they like for fish, meat and vegetables. What is sauce for the goose is sauce for the gander. Either perfect liberty should be allowed to everybody to do exactly as they like re trade, or the same restrictions should be placed on every industry and amusement in the United Kingdom and Ireland.

I am, &c.,

North Country

A WINEGROWER'S SACRIFICE

SIR – In the inspiring appeal which the Bishop of London sends to his people he thus differentiates between 'Traitor' and 'Patriot':

'Am I making what I can out of the war?'

'Am I giving up all I can to the common cause?'

The answer to these questions, he says, marks the traitor from the patriot.

The civilised world has been shocked during the last few days by the deplorable exhibition of self-interest amongst a certain section of the community, and one finds comfort in the numberless instances of self-sacrifice and devotion to the Motherland that are being displayed amongst our kinsmen many thousands of miles away. It has required no oratory from a cabinet minister to bring home to these splendid fellows the needs of the Empire; at the slightest hint of danger their patriotism has shamed those few in England who have put their own in the needs of their country. Let me instance one such case which has come before me in the Australian mail received this morning.

A young winegrower, but recently married, offered himself for the war. He came some hundreds of miles from his up-country vineyard for examination at Melbourne, and was declined owing to the fact that he had two protruding toes –

the effect of over-tight boots in his youth. He inquired of the doctor if they would take him were the offending toes removed. The answer was affirmative. This young fellow went straight away to a private hospital, and had the operation performed. Upon again presenting himself he was accepted, and now, as an officer in the Australian contingent, will be in England in a few days. I would like to mention his name, but he is a gentleman, and would resent it. I know the family well.

This country is teeming with men who are placing – or are prepared to place – themselves at the service of England at any self-sacrifice. Men such as these weld our great Empire together.

Born, and bred under its glorious sunshine, our Australian kinsmen may be careless as to discipline, but they have such abundance of life and vigour and energy of brain as to render them amongst the greatest assets of the Empire.

I am, Sir, yours faithfully,

P.B. Burgoyne
Broadlands, Ascot

WASTE IN HOTELS

SIR – As I am constantly reading about retrenchment, I should like to mention an instance of the enormous waste of food daily taking place in the large hotels of this country. Two or three months ago I was staying at one of London's largest hotels, and I should like to mention one of many such incidents.

The meal, breakfast, 8s 6d, table d'hôte. Six people sitting at the next table. First, a large dish of fish; half sent back, dirty plates being put on the top of the food. Then a dish of ham and eggs, twelve eggs for the six people. Only four of these eggs and a small proportion of the ham was eaten. The remainder served in the same way as the uneaten fish, namely, dirty plates placed on the food to enable the waiter to carry it away more easily.

This happens, as every hotel frequenter knows perfectly well, over and over again daily in every large hotel in England. Why? Because people for 3s 6d are allowed to order whatever they like and far more than they can eat. If they had to pay for each course separately it is possible people would order only what they really required. Possibly in some cases it may be from thoughtlessness, but notices ought to be placed in all hotels calling visitors' attention to it, and all table d'hôte meals stopped.

Yours truly,

M.D.

26 July 1915

GERMAN MUSIC

SIR – Will you kindly spare me a few lines to reply to the letter from Mr David Wood in today's *Daily Telegraph*? Mr Wood does not seem to realise the point at issue. In their action at the Palladium on 9 May the London Symphony Orchestra were guilty of a wanton outrage on Wagner's memory. What possible connection could there be between the sinking of the *Lusitania* and the tender beauty of the 'Siegfried Idyll'? The barring of all German music till after the war – however foolish and unnecessary – could be understood, but on 9 May the programme included Mendelssohn's 'Violin Concerto'. Now, as Mr Wood will not need to be told, Mendelssohn and Wagner belonged to the same generation. Mendelssohn was born in 1809 and Wagner in 1813. The 'Violin Concerto' is not more remote than the 'Siegfried Idyll' from present horrors. In this matter of justice to Wagner in wartime our musical leaders, with the exception of Mr Ashton Ellis, have been silent. Hence the intrusion of a mere camp follower.

I am, Sir, yours, &c.,

Sydney H. Pardon
80 Fleet Street, E C.

P.S. I notice that at the forthcoming Promenade Concerts the Queen's Hall Orchestra will be on the side of generosity and fair play.

4 August 1915

THE FIGHT FOR RIGHT

A Holy War

SIR – Fundamentally – in the last resort – all depends upon spirit. Organisation is only a means for bringing spirit into effect. A machine is the means to employ for utilising energy. It is the steam in the engine and the spirit in the national organisation that is the important thing.

Shells are necessary, but they are useless without the energy in the gun to propel them. Guns are required, but the man behind the gun is more important than the gun. Millions of men are wanted, but their value is in their spirit, and in the spirit of the nations which sends them and upholds them. It is the spirit that matters. And the spirit of the nation should be the affair of its spiritual leaders.

Especially in the present war is attention to the spirit called for. As the Prime Minister says, it is a spiritual conflict – a conflict between the German spirit and the spirit which animates us. The future of the world is at stake. If the Germans win, the German spirit will dominate human affairs for ages to come. German necessity will know no law. Belgiums will be trampled on; *Lusitanias* will be submarined. All who oppose will be either poisoned, or, with liquid fire, scorched off the earth. No considerations of honour, of humanity, or of anything else will stand in the way. 'Woe to the vanquished,' the Kaiser has said. The German will and German *Kultur* alone will be permitted.

What we are fighting for is that German necessity shall know law – the law of right – and, what is more, shall obey it. We are fighting that the rights of Serbia, Belgium and every other state, small or great, shall be respected. We are fighting that the ordinary human rights of defenceless women and children and of unarmed civilians shall be preserved. We are engaged in a spiritual conflict – a holy war – the Fight for Right.

This fight we have to win. But to win those of us who are able must stir the spirit of the people, summon up all the spiritual forces of the nation, collect those energies together and direct them on to the one great end we have in view – the maintenance of human right.

And not merely quantity of spiritual energy is required, but quality also. The Germans have unsurpassed organisation and immense spirit behind it. But the quality of their spirit is gross. It is the spirit of the beast, not of the man. Ours must be different, and our finest spirits must refine it till it is of the best. And, fortunately, the finest is also the strongest and most enduring.

Meetings on Sundays

Now it is in the assembling of ourselves together for some high purpose that spiritual energy is generated. There human touch is felt, elbow to elbow and heart to heart; and something higher emerges than the individuals in isolation possess. There, too, the multitude has the opportunity of being influenced by the best, and the best have a chance of making their influence felt. And for assemblings for so sacred a purpose as maintaining the right what more fitting occasions than those offered by our Sundays could be found?

What I would urge, then, is that on Sundays meetings should be held (at times not interfering with the usual church services) on ground common to the whole community – in the open air, the town hall or other public building – and that the spiritual nature of this conflict be impressed upon the people. And these meetings might be addressed by laymen as well as by ministers; by women as well as by men; by members of the congregation as well as by occupants of the platform. The whole idea would be to make the call felt by each and to let the spirit come out where and when it will that it may communicate itself to others.

Every means – music, speech, song, the recital of the great words of others, the examples of men and women of today – should be used to arouse the spirit of the people, and appeal be made to their highest and not to their lowest sentiments – not to self-interest, fear, hate, revenge, but to self-sacrifice and that devotion to country and to kind which gives up all that the world may be a better place for those who follow after.

And that something practical might eventuate, those who are willing to offer themselves for service to their country might be asked to present themselves at the close of the meeting, and they might then be directed by competent advisers to where their own particular services might be used with fullest effect. Recruits – and free and willing recruits – for every department of the country's service would then come forward, and every single one would have felt the great call on him and his spirit rising to the call. He would ever after feel an abhorrence of all that hindered his answering it to the full, and he would be possessed of a determination to do his best in his own little line to carry the great cause forward till the Fight for Right is won.

I am, Sir, your obedient servant,

Francis Younghusband
3 Buckingham Gate, S.W.

———

6 August 1915

APPEAL BY MR G.K. CHESTERTON

Relief in Belgium

SIR – I hope you will grant me space to say a few words about the Belgians still in Belgium. The admirable efforts of the National Committee for Relief in Belgium are going a long way to avert famine, but if the million and a half destitute Belgians are to be kept alive the National Committee must have yet further support. The only conceivable cause of doubt in the matter must lie in a mere weariness in well-doing, produced not by any intellectual difficulty, but by such wholly unintellectual things as time and fatigue. I think, therefore, the best way of preventing any possible neglect of so great a matter is to repeal once more the great truths upon which rested the whole original claim, not so much on our sympathy as on our common honesty. The simplicity and enormity of the Belgian story can best be set forth, perhaps, in four truisms, all toweringly self-evident.

First, of course, the mere badness of the story is almost too big to be held in the mind. There have been stories of a woman or a child actually robbed of reason for life by the mere ocular shock of some revolting cruelty done in their presence. There was really a danger of something of the kind paralysing our protest against the largest and, by the help of God, the last of the crimes of the Prussian kings. The onlookers might have been struck into a sort of gibbering imbecility, and even amiability, by the full and indefensible finality of the foul stroke. We had no machine that could measure the stunning directness of the blow from hell. We could hardly realise an enormous public act which the actor did not wish to excuse, but only to execute. Yet such an act was the occupation of Belgium; almost the only act in history for which there was quite simply and literally nothing to be said. Bad history is the whole basis of Prussia; but even in bad history the Prussians could find no precedent and no palliation, and the more intelligent Prussians did not try. A few were so feeble-minded as to say they had found dangerous documents in Brussels, as if what they had done could possibly be excused by things they did not know when they did it. This almost piteous lapse in argument was, however, covered up by the cleverer Prussians as quickly as might be. They preferred to stand without a rag of reason on them than with such a rag as that. Before we came to the monstrous material suffering, there is in the existing situation an abstract unreason, nay an abstract insanity, which the brain of man must not bear. A nightmare must not abide to the end. The tiniest trace of Prussian victory that remains will make us think of something which is not to be thought of, of something like the victory of the beasts over mankind.

Second, it must be remembered that this murder has been done upon a people of such proximity and familiarity that there cannot be any mistake about the matter. There is some shadowy justification for the comparative indifference to the wrongs of very remote people, for it is not easy for us to guess how much slavery shocks a negro or cannibalism a cannibal. But the innkeepers and shopkeepers of Ostend felt exactly as the innkeepers and shopkeepers of Dover would feel. We have to imagine a prehistoric cruelty coming suddenly upon a scene which was civilised and almost commonplace. Imagine tigers breaking out of the Zoological Gardens and eating all the people in Albany Street, imagine Red Indians exhibited at Olympia literally scalping every passer-by from that place to Hammersmith Broadway; imagine Jack the Ripper crowned King of Whitechapel and conducting his executions in broad daylight outside the tube station at Aldgate; imagine as much as you can of what is violent and contradictory in an overturn of all modern life by troglodytes, and you are still falling short of the fearful Belgian scene in that familiar Belgian scenery. It is idle to talk of exaggerations or misrepresentations about a case so close to us. Chinese tortures may not be quite so fantastic as travellers tell us; Siberia may not be so desolate as its fugitives say it is; but we could no more invent such a massacre in Belgium than we could a massacre in Balham. The things of shameless shame that have been done are something worse than prodigies, worse than nightmares, worse than devilries; they are facts.

Third, this people we have heard of daily have endured this unheard of thing, and endured it for us. There are countless cases for compassion among the bewildering and heart-rending by-products of this war; but this is not a case for compassion. This is a case for that mere working minimum of a sense of honour that makes us repay a poor man who has advanced his last penny to post a letter we have forgotten to stamp. In this respect Belgium stands alone, and the claims even of other Allies may well stand aside till she is paid to the uttermost farthing. There has been self-sacrifice everywhere else, but it was self-sacrifice of individuals, each for his own country; the Serbian dying for Serbia, or the Italian for Italy. But the Belgian did not merely die for Belgium. Belgium died for Europe. Not only was the soldier sacrificed for the nation, the nation was sacrificed for mankind. It is a sacrifice which is I think, quite unique even among Christians; and quite inconceivable among pagans. If we even privately utter a murmur, or even privately grudge a penny for binding the wounds of so solitary and exceptional a martyr, we ourselves shall be something almost as solitary and exceptional. We shall perhaps be nearest to the state of that unspeakable sociologist who persuaded his wife to partake of a simultaneous suicide, and then himself cheerfully lived on.

Fourth: If there be anyone on this earth who does not find the final success of such crime more than the mind can bear; if there be anyone who does not feel it as the more graphic since it walks among the tramway lines and lamp-posts of a life like our own; if there be anyone who does not feel that to be caught napping about Belgium is like being caught robbing one's mother on her deathbed; there still remains a sort of brutal compassion for bodily pain, which has been half-admitted here and there even by the oppressors themselves. If we do not do a great deal more even than we have already done, it may yet be said of us that we left it to the very butchers of this nation to see that it did not bleed to death.

I, therefore, plead for further help for the members of the national committee who have taken this duty upon themselves. All subscriptions can be addressed to the treasurer at Trafalgar Buildings, Trafalgar Square, London, or to local committees where they have been formed.

Yours faithfully,

G.K. Chesterton
Overroads, Beaconsfield, Bucks

———

13 August 1915

BREAD FOR PRISONERS

A New Scheme

SIR – I have just returned from Switzerland, whither I was sent by the British Red Cross Society to ascertain whether, through that neutral channel, we could be of any further help to British prisoners in Germany.

Our society permits me to publish one recommendation which I have made, and which is to be acted upon at once. It relates to bread. There is no doubt whatever that most of the bread sent from this country to our prisoners through Holland arrives in an uneatable condition. I have seen hundreds of postcards to that effect, and have heard sufficient oral evidence to convince me that this is the fact.

On the other hand, the British section of the Prisoners' Help Society at Berne bakes and sends hundreds of loaves a week to our prisoners. These consignments reach the furthest camps in Germany in under five days, and always in first-rate condition. This is accounted for by the advantage in geographical position which Berne occupies, by the rapidity and regularity of transport, and by the special method of baking adopted by the bakers in Switzerland.

I therefore recommend to the Red Cross Society that, so far as they could secure it, no more bread should be sent direct from England to Germany; but that, instead, money should be sent to Mrs Grant Duff (wife of his Britannic Majesty's Minister at Berne, and representative in Switzerland of the British Red Cross Society) wherewith to buy flour wholesale at Marseilles, bake it in Berne and despatch it to our compatriots interned in Germany. This scheme has been adopted.

I suggest that this course should be followed by all committees and individuals now engaged in sending bread through other and less satisfactory channels. With their cheques (at the rate of 4s 6d for four weeks' bread for one man) they should also send to Mrs Grant Duff the names and full addresses of those to whom the parcels are to be despatched. By so doing they can ensure the arrival of the bread in an eatable condition through the agency of a most admirable and efficient organisation. All cheques should be made payable to Mrs Grant Duff, and addressed to her at the British Legation, Berne, Switzerland.

Your obedient servant,

Ian Malcolm (MP, Croydon)
British Red Cross Society, 83 Pall Mall, S.W.

———

19 August 1915

REGISTERING THE PEOPLE

Sir A. Spicer's Experience

SIR – As one of the many voluntary enumerators in connection with the National Registration Act, I think a personal experience may be of interest.

My area was in Hackney, and consisted of 193 houses. During Monday and Tuesday, 9 and 10 August, I distributed 744 forms amongst these houses; this will indicate the class of district. Many of the houses have two sets of occupants, and a few three. On Monday and Tuesday of this week I collected my forms, and, thanks to the interest displayed, I was enabled to complete my work, with four exceptions, by early evening.

Of course, there were misunderstandings on some points to be cleared up and put right, but the information enabling this to be done was readily given, and I cannot be too grateful for the help rendered.

One other word – I was much impressed by the number of families whose representatives have already gone to the colours or to the front, and there are, alas, not a few homes where they will never welcome again those who have gone and have given their lives for their King and country!

Yours faithfully,
Albert Spicer
10 Lancaster Gate, W.

4 September 1915

OUR VOLUNTEER CORPS

Sir A. Pinero's Appeal

SIR – Now that the resources of the nation in men and material are being mobilised and turned to account, one large and important asset is absolutely neglected and ignored by the authorities. The volunteers are a force 300,000 or 400,000 strong, disciplined, organised into battalions and brigades (called regiments), and subject to one central executive, the military member of which is a late Commander-in-Chief of the Army in India, General Sir O'Moore Creagh, VC, GCB, GCSI.

The men comprising it are mostly over military age; but Englishmen between forty and fifty, who have led active lives, are at least not more decrepit than Frenchmen, Germans or Austrians of equal age. And they are certainly capable of guarding railways, bases and internment camps, and would thus set free the large number of Regulars, Territorials and Reservists at present employed on these duties.

The Volunteers may be unequally trained. While some corps are certainly not far behind the battalions of the new armies in military training, others have not progressed beyond the drill ground, but all have some training and possess a knowledge of discipline.

Many are unarmed, but some battalions are fully equipped with Martini-Enfield rifles, such as the National Reserve carry today. Few are without enough rifles to arm their guards at least, and, indeed, for guard duty, particularly at night, shotguns or, better still, old Snider rifles with buckshot cartridges are preferable to rifles, inasmuch as a single bullet will miss its mark in the dark, and probably kill some innocent person at a distance, while shot, spreading wide and not carrying far, will catch the man aimed at.

Question of Control

The chief objection to the employment of volunteers is the fact that they are not 'attested', and consequently not subject to military authority. That difficulty can be easily removed. The volunteers are anxious to subject themselves to the provisions of military law during the time that they are doing duty, and, in case of imminent or actual invasion, they are desirous of being placed on exactly the same footing as Regular soldiers.

There is really no difficulty in making volunteers subject to the control of the military authorities. Every volunteer, having expressed his willingness to undertake duty, and having had his liabilities explained to him, can be detailed for guard or patrol and be under military discipline from the hour that he is ordered to the hour when he is dismissed at the conclusion of his duties. Legislation is hardly necessary for this. An order from the Army Council, through the Central Association of Volunteer Training Corps, is sufficient.

While we are busily discussing how best to deal with the 'slacker,' there are 300,000 or 400,000 men eagerly waiting for some call upon their services. Their willingness to serve goes unheeded, and no one seems able to force the question to the front.

When the Volunteer Training Corps movement was first mooted, the War Office seemed to apprehend that it would interfere with recruiting for the Regular Army, that shirkers would shelter themselves inside a Volunteer uniform and claim that they were 'doing their bit'. But these Volunteer Training Corps have proved the finest recruiting ground that the Army has got, and send to it at least partially, if not fully, trained men. The 1st Battalion (United Arts Rifles) Central London Volunteer Regiment has supplied 100 officers and 200 to 300 men to the Services. Some of them have already fallen in action. The 3rd Battalion (Old Boys) Central London Volunteer Regiment has supplied over 400. And it is the same tale throughout the country. Men who have no liking for military life make a trial of the Volunteers, acquire that liking, and join the colours.

I am, Sir, yours faithfully,

Arthur Pinero, Chairman United Arts Rifles
115a Harley Street, W.

———

4 October 1915

'MAKERS OF HISTORY'

SIR – In your issue of 1st inst. I notice that you inserted a letter from my son, Lance-Corporal J.W. Ranson, No. 16469, B. Co., 1st Suffolk Regiment, and I wish to correct your introduction to the same. I regret to say that my son is not now serving at the front, having been reported missing since Whit Monday night, and I am unable to trace him.

Should this or my son's letter meet the eye of any of your readers who could give me some information as to what happened to my boy upon that night, I would feel greatly obliged.

Yours faithfully,

Jos Ranson
69 Ravenslea Road, Wandsworth Common, S.W.

————

12 October 1915

PRAYERS FOR THE FORCES

Bishop Taylor Smith's Appeal

SIR – It is now nearly fifteen months since the call to prayer at noon on behalf of our soldiers, sailors and airmen was first responded to. The universal midday prayer meeting has not only been a source of strength and comfort to our fighting men at the front, of which I have ample evidence, but it has proved a bond of union between all Christian folk throughout the Empire.

May I once again invoke the powerful influence of the *Daily Telegraph* on behalf of those of our troops who have still to go forth, as well as for those who shall return?

I tremble for the Church that does not set aside at this time all that does not matter, and give herself to this unique opportunity to evangelise and help spiritually the men whose hearts and minds are awakened towards the things which are unseen and consequently eternal.

It has been my prayer and hope for some years now that the Army might become the greatest missionary society the world has ever known.

A nation with such a consecrated body of men – in the Services today and in civil life tomorrow – would prove an irresistible force against all the powers of evil.

I plead for more prayer on behalf of our soldiers, sailors and airmen.

I am, Sir, yours faithfully,

J. Taylor Smith, Bishop-Chaplain-General
War Office

14 October 1915

GAME FOR THE WOUNDED

Needs of London Hospitals

SIR – Once again we would ask you to assist us in bringing to the notice of those who are now shooting the need in the London hospitals for game for the wounded. For the last two months, owing to the generosity of those who have answered our appeal, we have received close upon 3,000 brace of grouse, partridges and pheasants; over 150 hares and rabbits, together with many haunches of venison. But we need more.

If only those who have helped us so far could realise how much their gifts are appreciated by the wounded they would, we feel sure, help us to satisfy the daily requests that we receive for more. It is, of course, only natural that those who have game to dispose of should satisfy the wants of the town or country hospitals in their own locality. Unfortunately, in the process the many hundreds of wounded officers and men in the metropolitan hospitals are less well remembered. To those who have game to dispose of, therefore, we would ask that a percentage, no matter how small, should be sent to us for distribution among the London hospitals. By this means, the wounded soldiers in town and country would benefit alike.

In putting forward this earnest request we would point out that ample arrangements have been made for distributing such gifts, and if they are sent to Mr T. Comyn Platt, hon.

secretary, 1900 Club, 3 Pickering Place, St James's, London, they will be gratefully acknowledged. As it is hoped that this further appeal will be generously responded to, we would ask those sending game to help us still further by paying the carriage of such gifts.

Yours truly,

(Signed),

Selborne
Edward Carson
Charles Beresford
Alexander Henderson
W.C. Bridgeman
J.A. Grant
Basil E. Peto
Guy Pym

———

22 October 1915

SWEATERS FOR THE TROOPS

SIR – Will you kindly give me room to say that, with the approval of the War Office, I propose to carry on my undertaking of last winter to dye for the troops any sweaters sent me, and hand them over to the proper quarter.

On the whole, sweaters seem the most useful garment of all to send. If there are not more sweaters for me to clean and dye will not some of your readers try their kind and clever hands at knitting them?

Last winter I was able to send out over 13,000, and the supplement of smaller comforts kindly sent to help fill up the sacks brought the total number up to nearly 20,000. Let us see what we can manage this year.

Yours faithfully,

John Penoyre
8 King's Bench Walk, Inner Temple, E.C.

CARDS FOR THE TROOPS

SIR – One of the greatest resources of our wounded heroes in their weary hours is a game of cards, and there is a demand from our hospitals in Flanders, in Malta and Egypt, and wherever our soldiers are being cared for, for spare packs of cards from home.

The Court of the Worshipful Company of Makers of Playing Cards has been approached on the matter, and has very willingly agreed to make an appeal to the public, through the powerful aid of the Press, for their generous help by forwarding to us (1) packs of cards, whether new or partially used, and (2) money for the purchase of cards, which the company can secure on trade terms.

Packs of cards and donations may be sent to W. Hayes, Esq., J.P., Master of the Playing Card Makers' Company, Guildhall, London E.C.

This appeal is made with the express approval of the Lord Mayor.

Yours faithfully,

(Signed) William Hayes, Master
Harry S. Foster, Past Master
John Farrer, Senior Warden
A.K. Barlow, Junior Warden
Worshipful Playing Card Makers' Company, Guildhall, E.C.

———

23 October 1915

ENEMY ALIENS IN MOTOR CARS

SIR – Some few weeks ago I reported that a naturalised German with a German wife, who had been chauffeur to the Kaiser when on a visit to this country, and had remained here after the Kaiser's return, was now keeping a garage at Penrith, which a glance at the map will show is a point that, besides being on one of the high roads between England and Scotland, presents possibilities for observation, with the aid of a car, on both east and west coasts. Having heard nothing of the matter since I made my report, I motored to Penrith to see how it stood, and found that the German in question was still running the garage, though it was no longer advertised under his name.

That any German, whether naturalised at not, should be allowed to run a garage in time of war is, I submit, indefensible, and why it has been permitted is beyond comprehension.

Further than this, I venture to assert that the time has arrived when no enemy alien, whether naturalised or not, should be permitted to be in possession of a private car, for there can be no doubt that the indiscriminate use of motor cars without any check or restriction affords opportunities to enemy aliens to undertake activities which may be greatly prejudicial to this country.

How this works may be seen from a recent experience of my own. Last week, in motoring from Castle Douglas to Blackburn, I passed important works (for ammunition, I believe) without any challenge whatever. There was apparently nothing to prevent me making observations or taking photographs, if I had wished to do so. Surely I ought to have been stopped, and the authorities should have satisfied themselves as to who and what I was.

It will no doubt be objected that such stoppage would be a grave inconvenience to users of motors. So it might be in time of peace, but we are at war and cannot afford to sacrifice any precaution.

I would, therefore, suggest that no enemy alien, naturalised or other, should be permitted to be in possession of a car during the war; and I would further urge that in the case of genuine British subjects of British race a special permit to own and use a car, to be issued by the defence authorities, should be made obligatory.

Yours, &c.,

Robert Yerburgh
Carlton Club, S.W.

————

25 October 1915

APPEAL TO THE CHURCHES

SIR – Our hearts are too full for us to say all that we feel about the martyrdom of Miss Edith Cavell, but I venture to suggest that a day be appointed by the various authorities concerned, on which a memorial service should be held in every church and chapel of all denominations (according to the accustomed forms of all sections of religious opinion) in memory of this noble lady done to death by the ministers of Satan in Belgium, at which her death should be solemnly presented in prayer before the most High, and the whole German nation solemnly called to judgment before the Throne of God. Personal and national vengeance is to be deprecated. 'Mihi vindicta, ego retribuam dicit Dominus', and this is still the Christian rule, but against the verdict of history and civilisation no race group can make successful appeal. Doubtless such a memorial would be widely observed in America.

Yours faithfully,

J. Plowden-Wardlow
St Edward's Vicarage, Newnham, Cambridge

———

1 November 1915

NAME FOR A LONDON STREET

SIR – Permit me to suggest that London should without delay follow the example of Paris and rename some street after the brave lady whose murder we so bitterly lament.

The site on which the New Nurses' Home in Whitechapel is to be erected is bordered on one side by Oxford Street, E., a name which is continually being confused with the great thoroughfare farther west. To change this into Cavell Road would be a graceful act on the part of the London County Council, and would at the same time be a useful improvement.

I am, yours faithfully,

A. Marshall Jay
17 Old Broad Street, E.C.

2 November 1915

STRANDED AT VICTORIA

The Return of Our Soldiers

SIR – There arrived at Victoria Station on Saturday last, at about 2.30 a.m., about 1,300 tired officers and men, home from the front on four days' leave.

And there, in the cold and miserable morning, they were left stranded, without any facilities for getting away to their homes in London or to the various stations to continue their journeys to the provinces. No conveyances of any kind were available, and the only place of refreshment open was the VAD coffee stall in the corner of the station. The ladies there did everything possible, but it was totally beyond their power to supply 1,300 men in the very small place allotted to them.

So these men, after weary months in the trenches, came home for four days, and that is the welcome we gave them. We landed them at Victoria at the very worst hour of the morning, without food or shelter or means of getting home; and there they had to herd in the station for hours until the omnibuses and trains began to run. I understand the same thing is happening every day. It is a poor return for all they have done, and are doing, for us; and I think something should be done at once.

There is at Victoria Station a large hall underground, and if nothing better can be arranged I suggest that the hall be opened to the arriving men, a good fire lighted, and that the VAD stall should be set up in the hall, so that the men could assemble there in the warmth and light and with the possibility of getting some light refreshment, until such time as they can get away to their homes.

The cleaning of the hall and the fire would entail some little expense, but that would be so very slight as compared with the comfort of the men that it is not worth considering.

If this matter can be arranged I will undertake to provide a fair share of the expense, and if possible the whole of it.

I am, Sir, yours faithfully,

Billeter
London E.C.

———

THE BAN OF THE LIBRARIAN

No Fiction in Wartime

SIR – We live in sad and dull days. The Library Committee of the Wandsworth Borough Council has, with the instincts of a public undertaker, decided to add to this depression by placing a ban on the circulation of all works of fiction to adult or juvenile during the period of the war. What is the motive – economy, or a desire to strip us of anything that may give a change to thought? My lad wants to read *Coral Island*. I may not revel in the delights of *Pamela, or Virtue Rewarded*.

In sheer desperation I have been driven to the literature of the law. I have, for instance, gambolled in the sunshine of *Torts*. *Coke upon Littleton* has been my charm, and I have passed on to Halsbury's *Laws of England*, with *The Institutes of Justinian* as a delicate snack.

At this moment of parochial dictation, I shall, with the permission of those enlightened folk who govern me, pass on to brighter fare, and perforce, ponder over *The Literature of the Graveyard*, *Meditations among the Tombs*, *Dr Blair's Sermons*, Bunyan's *Holy War*, and Fox's *Book of Martyrs*. And when I am satiated with this inspiriting fare I shall delve into *Notes on a Case of Self-inoculation with the Bacillus Aerogenes Capsulatus*, and close my researches with a work dealing with *Investigation of the Brain and Nervous System*, in order, if possible, to discover the genesis of the stupid decision to which, with your permission, I venture to draw attention. I wonder what the late Sir George Newnes, the donor of the library, would think of this official action?

Yours, &c.,

E.P.N.
Putney

———

3 November 1915

BAN OF THE LIBRARIAN

Fiction in Wartime

SIR – Your correspondent 'E.P.N.' must be a very subtle humourist. To begin with, though our days are sad, they are by no means 'dull'. At the present crisis there is no excuse for being dull for want of something to read. No fiction can have such brilliant interest as the realities furnished by the daily papers. The youngster who is thirsting for *Coral Island* might safely be directed to your own pages of today, and, with the assistance of maps and an occasional glance at the encyclopedia would be entertained, as well as assisted in his intellectual development. As to the iniquity of the Wandsworth Borough Council, and the stupid instincts of the Library Committee, the process of restriction which 'E.P.N.' complains of is only part of the great plan of self-denial and economy to which we have been called in these 'sad' times. It is not our business to complain of petty deprivations. It is even possible to derive profit from this chastening. And to make a grievance of what is already harassing the librarians and other officials is not worthy of a true citizen.

So, I would not have 'E.P.N.' give way to discontent. Happy indeed is he if he can find solace in Dr Blair or Lord Halsbury, or 'Justinian'. Fortunate indeed is he if his own personal anxieties arising from the war do not entirely preclude some sympathy with others beside novel-readers!

Yours obediently,

Edward Smith
Wandsworth

THE LIBRARY RATE

SIR – I have read with interest the letter of 'E.P.N.' on the subject of the libraries in the borough of Wandsworth not issuing fiction during the period of the war. I understand from the librarians that it is owing to the small staff now employed (owing to enlistment, &c.) and for economy. I think 'E.P.N.' cannot have seen the crowds (especially on a Saturday) waiting for issue of novels, which was as much as the full staff could cope with. The lending department of one of the libraries in the borough has been closed entirely for several months, and I recently read that some boroughs are debating whether to close all their libraries entirely, or at any rate some of them.

It seems to me to be an occupation in which girls could well be employed, if it is only due to difficulty of obtaining assistants. Presumably if the libraries are to be closed the library rate will be dropped, or if partly closed the rate to be halved, but I have not heard of any suggestion of the kind yet.

Yours faithfully,

H.W.

———

A TIMELY PROTEST

SIR – Your correspondent, 'E.P.N.', who enters a timely protest against the decision of the Wandsworth Borough Council to stop the issue of fiction at its public libraries, has by no means exhausted the various classes of literature to which the rate-payers and their children will now be compelled to turn to pass the long winter evenings. There are, for instance, quite a number of interesting books on plumbing and grand opera, catalogues of coins, manuscripts, &c., in the British Museum; biographies of people little known and still less remembered; there are the poets and the other poets; and, last but not least, the Borough Council minutes.

What, it might be asked, has prompted the Council to ban fiction? It cannot be on the plea of economy, for the public library rate has not been altered. The only explanation would appear to be that the Council considers that this is no time for the reading of light literature, and so they propose to add to the gloom of our already gloomy lives.

I am, Sir,

E.J.F.
Putney

————

4 November 1915

MUNICIPAL EXPENDITURE

SIR – The Shoreditch Metropolitan Borough Council has just refitted its council chamber with elaborate new furniture at a cost of £750, and the National War Relief Fund has made a grant of half the amount for the employment of local men.

A more flagrant misapplication of local rates, local labour and national charity can hardly be conceived at the present crisis.

Yours truly,

W.C. Johnson
County Hall, Spring Gardens, S.W.

————

5 November 1915

PORRIDGE IN THE KITCHEN

SIR – On 1 November I consider the season of the year has arrived when porridge is desirable for breakfast, and have it served for my son and self. I told my cook to make porridge for the kitchen as well as the room. Result, one of my servants has given me notice because she considers such food is not fit to work on, and I quite expect the like reply from her fellow parlourmaid. I keep three indoor servants, and the family consists of my son and self, as stated above.

This is the outcome of trying to put into practice the Prime Minister's recommendation for wartime. I might mention that the porridge was to be followed by cold ham.

Yours faithfully,

Widower
London

---

8 November 1915

'CHRISTMAS IN WARTIME'

Albert Hall Bazaar

SIR – As president of the Prisoners of War Section of the Christmas in Wartime Bazaar, to be held at the Royal Albert

Hall on 8 December, under the patronage of Her Majesty the Queen, I appeal to the generosity of the public, which has never failed to accord its sympathy and support to any object which conduces to the comfort and well-being of our gallant soldiers and sailors.

At Christmas, when all our thoughts turn to all who are dearest to us; surely we shall not forget those who are cut off from the joys of home and family, and, having risked their lives in the service of their King and country, are now enduring the grievous penalty of imprisonment in a foreign land, where they suffer hardships in lieu of the affectionate care they have nobly merited.

The following articles have been suggested by the organisers of relief provided for our men in German prisons: socks, mufflers, &c., preserved foods of all kinds, cigarettes and smoking necessaries, games and plain Christmas cakes and puddings. If each housewife, in making preparations for her own family, would make one extra plain 3 lb pudding or cake and send it to the 'Christmas in Wartime', a double benefit would be conferred – a prisoner would have Christmas fare, and the Professional Classes War Relief Fund will be augmented.

It is proposed to have a number of parcels ready packed with the contributions received, in order that they may be purchased and despatched immediately to the prisoners.

Alice Princess Alexander of Teck
13–14 Prince's Gate, S.W.

9 *November 1915*

PRESS AND THE WAR

SIR – Your justly indignant article dealing with the false rumours regarding Lord Kitchener suggests an effective, if only partial, remedy for scaremongering. As the writer of the article remarks, the effect of last night's untrue announcement in London was instantaneous and disquieting. This was chiefly due to the rushing out of sensational bills by one or two evening papers. One was made to read, 'Lord Kitchener Resigns' – this in colossal letters, and merely upon the strength of a bald, unauthorised statement which obviously carried no weight. All the mischief, here in London at any rate, was caused by these placards. This is, of course, not an isolated instance; London streets have since the war began palpitated every afternoon and evening with spurious excitement fomented by the unholy competition of the fabricators of these pestiferous posters. Measures were taken in Paris early in the war to suppress the evil, but here at home it is allowed free play.

Why not stop the issue of all evening paper placards and prohibit the shouting out of news? This would involve no interference with the liberty of the press; all the latest intelligence would still be published, subject to censorship; the citizen could continue to buy his favourite evening paper; he would not be gulled into buying another against his will; our streets would be more tolerable in the matter of noises, and freer from unhealthy excitement; and we should all read the veritable news of the day in a properly balanced frame of mind. The comparatively sober and genuine contents bills of the morning papers might remain, but these mendacious copper-snatching réclame sheets should be suppressed, or, at any rate, strictly censored, until victory has been achieved, and perhaps after.

I am, yours obediently,

One Jealous of the Honour of the Press
London

MASSAGE FOR THE WOUNDED

SIR – May I be allowed, through the medium of your columns, to draw attention to the very pressing need for the treatment by massage and electricity for the wounded soldiers.

The Almeric Paget Massage Corps has been in existence since the beginning of the war, and is the official organisation, recognised by the War Office, for the supply of masseurs and masseuses for the military hospitals and convalescent camps throughout the United Kingdom.

The need for this form of treatment is increasing daily, and large camps are now being opened all over the county, besides those already in existence, where electrical and massage departments are to be a special feature. It is, therefore, necessary to procure the services of a very large number of masseuses, in addition to those already working on the corps, which now amount to about 700.

The qualifications, without which no application for enrolment on the Almeric Paget Massage Corps can be entertained, are:

1. A certificate of the Incorporated Society of Trained Masseuses; or
2. A certificate of a physical training college recognised by the Ling Association; or
3. A certificate of one of the public hospital schools of massage; or
4. A certificate dated prior to 1 January 1916, of any of the schools of massage approved by the War Office, provided that the candidate can produce two satisfactory references from qualified doctors who can speak from personal knowledge of the candidate's work and character at any time during the three years immediately preceding the date of application for enrolment on the corps.

Applicants should forward their names, addresses and qualifications as soon as possible to me at 39 Berkeley Square, London W.

Yours faithfully,

Essex French, Hon. Secretary, APMC
39 Berkeley Square, W.

13 November 1915

CARE OF HORSES IN WARTIME

Lady Smith-Dorrien's Appeal

SIR – This great European war is, I am well aware, taxing the charitable and patriotic to the very utmost; but there is one especially worthy object which, I submit, should not be overlooked, and that is the alleviation of the sufferings of our horses.

Without horses war could not be waged. Thus, apart from the humane side of the question, the reduction of wastage amongst them must be a matter of great moment to the cause. In 1912 'Our Dumb Friends League' started a branch called the Blue Cross Fund, which aimed at the care of horses in wartime.

This organisation is now firmly established, and has four large hospitals in France, which, opened at the commencement of the war, have not only widened their field of action, but have increased in efficiency during the past year. These hospitals have received full recognition from the French Government, and our offers of help for French horses have been gratefully accepted and freely taken advantage of. Indeed, some 2,000 wounded horses have been cured in our stables, the normal number of horses under our care being 600 or 700.

In addition to the care of animals, we have been able to supply large quantities of medicines, instruments, bandages, horse clothing, disinfectants, fly nets, &c., not only to mounted corps of the regular British and Indian and Territorial armies, but also to those raised for the help of the Empire by our great self-governing Dominions, the commanding officers of many of which have written most gratifying letters of thanks and appreciation.

Over £3,000 a month is needed to carry on this work on its present scale, and up to date we have received this amount from lovers of horses from all parts of the Empire. In view, however, of the extended duration of the war, the committee are naturally solicitous as to whether this flow of subscriptions can be maintained, and it is on this account I am making this further appeal for subscriptions, which may be sent to me addressed as follows: Lady Smith-Dorrien, president Blue Cross Fund, 58 Victoria Street, London S.W.

Yours truly,

Olive Smith-Dorrien
21 Eaton Terrace, S.W.

———

16 November 1915

EGGS FOR OUR WOUNDED

A Suburban Fowlhouse

SIR – Will you please grant me space for a few words in connection with the above important subject?

Soon after the war started I, with many others, realised that whilst our egg supply was bound to be enormously reduced, the demand, especially for our soldiers' and sailors' hospitals, would go up by leaps and bounds. So, as I am unfortunately about twenty-five years on the wrong side of the military age limit, I determined to do my utmost to supply some of this demand. For this purpose I erected a fowlhouse and run in my garden, purchased some pullets, and I am pleased to say during the last nine or ten months I have been able to send some hundreds of new-laid eggs to a large hospital in my neighbourhood. But I have been reckoning without my neighbour, who, incredible as it seems, and knowing as he does my purpose in keeping fowls, has called in the Borough Council inspector, who, though honestly admitting the perfect sanitary condition of both house and run and fowls, has – on the ground that the erection is a few inches higher than the legal height and a few inches nearer to a dwelling-house than the legal distance – ordered me to pull it down.

I do not propose to obey this order; at any rate, just yet, because I believe I read some weeks back that the Government are considering the best way to remove these very restrictions.

If that is so, I intend to defend my fort to the bitter end, in the hope that they may be able to hurry up to my assistance and to the assistance, I am sure, of many other citizens who are trying to help, and not like my curious neighbour, trying to hinder, our poor wounded lads. Strangely enough, my neighbour on the other side of me cannot do enough for my 'khaki' pullets, but saves all the household scraps for them. How different folk are.

Yours faithfully,

X
London

———

19 November 1915

THE KING'S EXAMPLE

A Duty of the Hour

SIR – This is a critical moment in our history, when every one of us would wish to share the sacrifice which our soldiers and sailors are making for their country. One way of sharing the sacrifice is by a self-denying economy. Our statesmen tell us that this is today a pressing national duty. Our current outlay of over four million a day on the war is, to use the Prime Minister's most recent words, 'gigantic and startling'. Economy, with prices rising all round, is no doubt difficult to effect. But there is one economy possible to almost all, which, if we will adopt it, would bring about an enormous reduction of national expenditure, yet one not taking from – indeed, adding to – our strength, and that is to abstain altogether from alcoholic drinks for ordinary use during the war. Six months ago our King challenged us by his own public example to do this. Our religious leaders have reputedly echoed the challenge. Why have so many of us been unresponsive? Surely, now that the appeal for national economy, to the point of personal sacrifice in every possible way, has gained an urgency obvious to everyone, the moment has more than come to effect this great saving for the common cause.

C. Oxon
Vernon Bartlet
A.J. Carlyle
H.S. Holland
T.H. Archer Houblon
W. Lock
Gilbert Murray
W. Osler
R.L. Ottley
L.R. Phelps
W.B. Selbie
Oxford

8 December 1915

COMFORTS FOR WELSH TROOPS

National Fund Appeal

SIR – The ever-growing number of Welsh soldiers, of which a very considerable proportion is now serving overseas, has added enormously to the claims upon the National Fund for Welsh Troops; and I have once again to appeal to the generosity and sympathy of all friends and well-wishers for a continuance of the aid that has been freely given to the National Fund since its inception. The letters received from commanding officers bear ample testimony to the value of the services rendered by the fund in adding to the comfort and well-being of Welsh troops, who have so gallantly responded to their country's call.

So far every requisition received has been complied with, but the work done hitherto is small compared with the needs of the present winter. Help can be given in various ways:

1. By subscriptions.
2. By contributions of comforts, particularly mufflers, mittens, socks, helmets and cardigan jackets.
3. By the purchase of the Welsh gift book, *Land of My Fathers*, which can be obtained from any bookseller or bookstall. It makes an ideal Christmas gift book.

The executive committee has recently been added to, and strenuous efforts are being made to make this fund in every way a national one, so as to cope with the overlapping and inequality of distribution of comforts which is productive of much waste and dissipation of energy.

All subscriptions and contributions of comforts may be addressed to me at 11 Downing Street, S.W.

Yours faithfully,

M. Lloyd George
11 Downing Street, London S.W.

———

9 December 1915

STRAY SOLDIERS' CHRISTMAS

SIR – Have any special arrangements been made for stray khakis on Christmas Day? This year as last, many thousands will be feasted and amused, but not all. I happened to spend the greater part of last Christmas Day in the Strand and at Victoria. I talked to two 'Princess Pat's', a man from Carlisle and one from the Tweed, among others. And the general opinion was, 'What a dull hole London is when you know no one, and have nowhere to go.'

Yours truly,

C. Sutcliffe Marriott
94 Boundary Road, N.W.

11 December 1915

THE CLERGY AND MILITARY SERVICE

SIR – The article which you have published today from Sir Malcolm Morris suggests certain considerations applicable to other fields than that which he traverses. He gives weighty reasons why young medical students should not be enlisted for the war, and I think his letter will carry conviction to many minds. It is absolutely necessary, in order that the medical service should be kept at its present high rate of efficiency, that young men should be allowed to finish their course, and that meanwhile they should be regarded as 'war workers' quite much as those who make munitions.

But can Sir Malcolm Morris's arguments be extended to other professions and departments of industry? Can they, for instance, be applied to the younger members of the priesthood? I know that here I am treading on rather dangerous ground, and that the problem has been rendered unnecessarily delicate by being mixed up with the question as to what Christianity means, and what is, or ought to be, its essential spirit. We shall only confuse plain issues if we insist on bringing in wider themes. We have not to deal with subjects of theory or philosophical estimates of the place of religion in a world system, but with plain, practical points which everyone can understand and appreciate. It is on this ground I venture to put aside the opinion, however dignified or magisterially expressed, of archbishops and other ecclesiastical authorities. They, no doubt, are technical experts in their way. But they rarely are men of the world or can give practical judgments on plain matters of fact.

My contention is that in the present crisis of our fate the younger clergy should, so far from being dissuaded or left to decide the matter according to their own consciences, be encouraged in every way voluntarily to offer themselves for military service. I suppose I need not argue this on grounds of civic duties – incumbent on every citizen of military age – nor yet justify the profession of arms as one of the highest of human callings. So long as patriotism is a virtue, it must in all senses be a noble and praiseworthy thing, in fact, a moral duty, to defend one's country in war; while the suggestion that a clergyman is 'a man of peace' need not embarrass us, considering that at the present moment the truest worshipper of peace is the man who is resolutely bent on prosecuting the campaign to the only legitimate and possible end.

Muscular Christianity

But there are two special reasons why young clergymen should enlist, one of which affects them and the other the older members of their calling. Let me begin with the second reason. It will not be denied, I imagine, that there are vast numbers of clergy of mature age who are quite able to discharge the duties of ministers of religion with admirable efficiency. I will go further. It is notorious that many of them are at present in penurious circumstances, while, at the same time, they are entitled on the score of character and work to preferment – in other words, to a better life wage. Surely this is a consideration which might weigh with the heads of a Church who are well aware on what a bare pittance some of the clergy – who have long since passed their youth – are forced to maintain themselves and keep up the status of gentlemen. If the younger members become soldiers, there will be more room left for earnest and conscientious men of mature age to earn on their life tasks in less needy circumstances. As for these younger members themselves, is there a single practical reason why they should not freely and joyfully offer themselves to fight their country's battles? They are young men, the red blood of youth flows in their veins, they have faith in the destiny of their race. Do they believe in goodness, and justice, and truth? Their country's cause is just, and good, and true. Are they Christians? Then for Heaven's sake let them gird their swords on their thighs and fight that Christ's Gospel be established on the ruins of the utterly Pagan and immoral creed of Prussia. For years the provost of Eton was a major commanding the Eton Volunteer Corps, which was technically called the 2nd Bucks Volunteer Battalion. I can imagine no finer example. To tell clergymen that they belong to a sacred order which exempts them from a citizen's duty is to tithe mint, and anise and cummin, and forget the weightier things of the law. It is to bid them acquiesce in a dominion of brutality and injustice and lust. War in a just cause is too fine an ideal for young clerics to neglect and pass by on the other side, as though it were none of their business. It was the Levite and the Pharisee who passed by on the other side when a wounded man was lying on their road.

Faithfully yours,

Emeritus
London

14 December 1915

THE CLERGY AND MILITARY SERVICE

Duty and Privilege

SIR – I agree with your correspondent 'Emeritus'. We are now face to face with first principles, and must not allow side issues to hide them. Is this war right or wrong? If it is right, if we have been forced into it, as the evidence most clearly shows, and the only alternative to fighting is to sit down under German dominance, i.e., under the rule of a country which has openly stated in the writings and words of its Emperor, generals and most distinguished professors that the only moral law it recognises in the government of a country is 'might is right' – then surely it is a duty and privilege for all men who are deserving of that highly valuable title to draw the sword, and not to leave it to others to do so for them.

How can clergymen ever hope to have any influence with their people in the future who have let slide the greatest opportunity a man can have – that of making 'the great sacrifice' for a noble cause? How can a clergyman in a Church which teaches self-sacrifice as the great Christian virtue tell his people to exhibit this principle, while he does not act on it himself? Let the clergy offer. Let the King decide on what kind of service they shall be sent.

Your obedient servant,

Archdeacon

LIONS OR LAMBS?

SIR – The Christian religion does two things:

1. It does as it would be done by.
2. It defends the weak.

If a clergyman on an open moor at midnight were attacked by two highwaymen and two of his brother clergymen were to appear on the scene, what would their duty be as Christians? It would be (1) to do as they would be done by, and (2) to defend the weak. Would it not? In that case their immediate duty would be to set to work to fight and vanquish the highwaymen, even if the fighting ended in death for one or more. That would be their plain duty, and they would do it – bishop or no bishop. If the two clergymen did not fight, they would act the part of the priest and the Levite in the parable of the Good Samaritan; and they would be the very kind of mean and miserable fellows whom Jesus held up to contempt and odium in that parable.

But if the victim of attack were not a clergyman but, say, a tailor, or a young girl, the Christian obligation to defend the one or the other would be just the same, would it not? How can any mere word logic set this plain thing of duty aside?

Well, then, was not weak and unoffending Belgium attacked by two strong highwaymen – Germany and Austria? Was not Franco attacked? Was not weak Serbia? Clearly it was Britain's duty as a Christian neighbour to defend those weak ones. Now the very same logic which makes fighting the clear duty of the unordained Christian – whom, however, St Paul describes as a 'King and a priest unto God' – makes it equally the duty of the ordained Christian priest. For, if Paul be right, the layman is as truly a priest as the clergyman. Any attempt to set up a standard of conduct and self-sacrifice for the ordained priest – and another and a higher standard for the unordained priest – has the appearance both of special pleading and unworthy shuffling; and it cannot but recoil disastrously, not only on the clergy, but on the Church of England as a whole.

Many months ago I wrote a letter urging that if five of six thousands of the younger clergy would join the fighting ranks they would do more good to Christianity and the mother church than all the sermons of all the clergy preached throughout the war. That opinion I still adhere to, and as a former churchwarden, of ten years' standing, I beg the younger clergy to lay it to heart. The bishops, I fear, want them to act as lambs, whereas the real need of the time is for British lions, and as many of them as we can get.

Your obedient servant,

Geo. W. Potter, MD
London

WORK OF THE CHURCH

SIR – Your correspondent 'Emeritus' seems to be one of those vast number of people who are totally ignorant of the 'office and work of a priest in the church of God'. I would suggest to him that it would be helpful to him if he were to make a study of the office for the ordering of priests in the Prayer Book, and also study the whole history of the priesthood from the earliest times.

He is evidently, too, one of those people who feel no need of spiritual ministrations, or he would feel for many who are deprived of such help by the shortage of clergy even in normal times; and such shortage is becoming more and more serious during this time of war. There are more and more homes each day into which anxiety, sorrow and bereavement are entering, and it is part of the office and work of a priest to bear to each home and each individual the message of comfort and hope which comes from God alone, and to give them the strength of God, which alone can support them, and which He has entrusted to his Church to convey.

But, apart from this, there is the fact that the Church throughout the ages has always laid down the principle that one who is solemnly ordained to minister the Sacraments must not shed blood – even David was not allowed to build the temple because he had shed blood; how much more one who is to minister at the altar, and must give his whole life entirely and solely to his sacred function.

Men who take holy orders are expected to be men of honour, and in asking them to forsake their sacred work for combatant service your correspondent is asking them to abrogate a great principle, and to break their oath taken before God at the most solemn moment in their lives.

Finally, there are abundant signs that the nation has forsaken God in recent years, and if the nation is to deserve victory she must be brought back to her allegiance to God, and it is again part of the office and work of a priest to do this. 'Emeritus' must realise that the nation is being tried; and if she is to come out of her trial purged as through fire she must adhere to the twofold principle laid down by our Lord, and not leave one or the other undone – 'Render unto Caesar the things that are Caesar's, and to God the things that are God's.'

Faithfully yours,

A Young Priest

NO RENUNCIATION OF MANHOOD

SIR – I believe at present the congregations in many churches are unusually small, and the clergy are casting about for the reason of this falling away from the good attendances in the first few months of the war. Is it not probable that many people are feeling that the clergy seem much more anxious to point out other people's duties to them than to do their own?

Other clergy and ministers renounce no privileges of British manhood. Why, then, should they shirk the duties, when those involve hardship and danger? I am afraid that plain people will be very little impressed by the subtleties of learned bishops and archbishops when they look at a healthy unmarried curate staging at home in safety and comfort, and sheltering himself behind a possible reading of the Ordination Service. The women whose menfolk are doing a man's part have no use for this peculiar 'third sex' which the bishops seem to wish to create.

A Soldier's Mother

HOMES OF THE CLERGY

SIR – 'Emeritus' hits the bull's-eye. The bishop misses the target. The question today is not the standing of the clergy. The question, looked at by the lurid fires of Belgium, is: Are the families and homes of the clergy worth saving? If not, the bishop is all right; if they are, a much higher authority than the whole bench of bishops combined has put sacrifice on a far higher plane than service; see St John 15:16.

Only a Layman

THE DICTATES OF CONSCIENCE

SIR – Every broad-minded man who read your issue of Saturday last must appreciate the remarks of 'Emeritus'. Surely if there is any body of men placed under an obligation to fight for the 'Right', it is that body so often preaching about it. Nay, should not the clergy welcome this opportunity, that they may regain the confidence of the manhood of this country, which, judged by the congregations now supporting them, they have to a very large extent lost.

Let every young priest follow the dictates of his conscience; let him ask himself honestly what his Master would have him do, remembering always that for a lasting peace of mind it will be far better, if not easier, to flout his bishop than his conscience.

The Anglican Church is an established church. The State she is sometimes proud to recognise as her handmaid. What will she do today? Will she spill the blood of her sons to uphold that handmaid which, a few months ago, she was so tenaciously clinging to, or will she emblazon her banner with 'disloyalty' and 'ingratitude!'?

Yours, &c.

Caliban

PRACTICAL ECONOMY

Advice to the Public

SIR – The cry of 'economy' at the present moment is well-nigh deafening, upon all sides, and the public may be pardoned if they become confused as to its meaning, or puzzled as to what economy really is. We are beginning to lose sight of the fact that the extremist, whatever attitude he assumes, or whatever cause he supports, defeats his own object.

It is safe to assert, speaking broadly, that at all times the spendthrift is more useful to the nation than the miser. His life may be a short and merry one, yet he injures none but himself, the community benefiting by the diffusion of his money; whereas it is clear that the hoarder not only sacrifices by his parsimony the pleasures and moat of the necessaries of life, but injures the nation by secreting wealth which in the ordinary course would circulate freely and assist other men to live.

Naturally, I do not wish to prove that we should all become reckless, spending our money broadcast; but it is obvious from a commercial and material point of view that a moderate middle course is best. If, say, a businessman or private person owns an article of any given value, and another person wants it, and has that amount available and lying idle, the wiser method is to exchange. The seller is then enabled to employ the money for purposes of commerce, paying his workmen, purchasing necessaries from other tradesmen, &c., and these in their turn circulate the money and assist in maintaining the revenue of the country.

Indiscriminate Retrenchment

In the name of economy – falsely so-called – many people are trying to repress and to cripple ordinary commercial or business transactions such as I have instanced above; their intentions may be of the best, but their policy is short-sighted and illogical. Followed to its reasonable conclusion, it does away with the very means of producing national resources for the continuance of this war.

Lord Milner his said, very rightly, that any criticism which is to be of service must be constructive. May I then suggest that our new-born passion for retrenchment should be wisely controlled, and not indiscriminate, as it seems to be at the moment? Economy moderately practised is praiseworthy, since it results naturally in sounder financial conditions; economy run mad is simply disastrous.

The principal points to bear in mind and to emphasise in authoritative advice to the spending classes are: (1) Purchase, whenever possible, British goods only; (2) live within your means, saving a portion – however small – of income, in order to invest in War Loan stock, also to have a reserve for the proverbial rainy day; (3) in cutting down expenses remember that the money you spend forms the basis of other people's savings, therefore to carry economy to extremes damages your neighbour, is selfish and is unpatriotic.

If this policy which I have thus briefly outlined were judiciously followed the majority of people would manage to pay their way honourably through this crisis. And, finally, there would be no lack of investors when the next demand arises for funds to carry on this battle for England's stability and security.

I am, Sir, yours faithfully,

G. Booth Heming
London

NO HONOURS FOR S.W. AFRICA

SIR – The lists of honours awarded for valiant exploits in sundry theatres of the war have been read with satisfaction by the public; they have brought much gratification to the friends of officers and men who have been decorated.

Is it not passing strange that not a single honour has been given in respect of the one complete and successful campaign as yet accomplished?

The danger and the stress of the South-West Africa campaign were appalling. Many officers and men who fought and won are now on the eve of starting to share fresh perils. Is there to be no recognition of what they have already done?

Yours faithfully,
A Friend

15 December 1915

THE CLERGY AND MILITARY SERVICE

Value as Officers

SIR – Could not clergy be enlisted as officers, and so give service to their country? The duty of officers is mainly to instruct the men, and to lead them on, and to inspire them in the battle. Sometimes they are not armed themselves, or only have some weapon for defence, but they are examples of pluck and courage, and if they are, as they should be, men respected for example, and trusted for sound judgment, they are readily followed by their men, who will dare, and if need be die, under their leadership.

Besides this, a clergyman should have a healthy influence amongst other officers, and need not lose any part of his sacred calling by serving in the equally sacred cause of resisting wrong and contending for the right. The clergy, more than most men, are accustomed to command and instruct, so that the duties they would have, as officers in the Army, would be quite congenial to them.

Yours faithfully,

Canon

OBEDIENCE OR CONSCIENCE

SIR – The letter of 'Emeritus' in your issue of 11 December puts very forcibly the arguments in favour of military service for the clergy, but inasmuch as it leaves out of sight the main argument on the other side, it is liable to give a wrong impression. The younger clergy do not need any encouragement to serve their country at such a time as this. All they need is permission, and so long as that is withheld they are not free to go, however willing and anxious they may be to do so.

The real fact is – and it is not as well known as it should be – that the clergy are bound by their ordination vows to obey their bishop, and so long as the bishops refuse to give permission to serve, the clergy are hopeless in the matter. Every clergyman at his ordination, whether as priest or deacon, has to answer this question: 'Will you reverently obey your ordinary and other chief minister, unto whom is committed the charge and government over you: following with a glad mind and will their godly admonitions, and submitting yourself to their godly judgments?' And the answer to the question is given in these words: 'I will so do, the Lord being my helper.'

Now – whether this is technically equivalent to an oath or not – it is certain that any man who diverted from this requirement would be refused ordination; it is one of the express conditions on which he receives his commission, and if so, he is certainly not at liberty to disregard it on any ground of private judgment. For if he is, then there is clearly an end of all order and discipline in the Church.

Whether the bishops are right or not in the attitude they have taken up is open to question. There are probably many besides myself who gravely doubt the wisdom of their decision. But that does not in the least alter the fact that, so long as the bishops are of their present mind in the matter, so long will it be impossible for the clergy to offer themselves for the service of their King and country, as many of them are longing to do.

The letter of 'Emeritus' seems to assume that the decision is left to the conscience of the individual, but in this he is mistaken. All that is left to the conscience of the individual is the question whether it is right for a clergyman to bear arms – and on this there may well be differences of opinion – but so long as the clergy are not free to bear arms, under the terms of their commission, argument on this point must be purely academic. It is rumoured that the bishops themselves are not of one mind on the subject, but this does not appear officially, and until they give official permission to the clergy to offer themselves for service, it is only fair to the latter to remember that they are absolutely prohibited from doing so.

Clericus

'ONCE A PRIEST, ALWAYS A PRIEST'

SIR – The fact that a man has in common with many another lost one of two sons in the war cannot excuse him exploiting his animus against the Church of England by making a cowardly anonymous attack upon her clergy. He, and such as he, may be reminded of the Divine injunction to 'Render therefore unto Caesar the things which are Caesar's, and unto God the things that are God's', and in this light to read the Ordinal, for which purpose a prayer book can easily be borrowed.

The Church of England, being a part of the Catholic Church, naturally accepts the principle laid down by the Church from the first, that men in holy orders shall not bear arms – a principle which must surely recommend itself to all thinking people who have any regard for the fitness of things. Against this seemly principle the opinions of individual bishops are absolutely valueless. Cases that can be quoted of militant prelates only provide instances of flagrant violation of the rule.

While it is, of course, common knowledge that military service was forced on French priests by an anti-Christian State, one has to learn on better authority than that of your fatherly correspondent that the Roman clergy of any other nation are serving as combatants. And our younger clergy will doubtless be quite content to be classed as 'the meanest of shirkers' in such noble company as that of the Eastern, and notably the Russian, clergy, whose ministrations to the troops are recognised as such an energising asset.

Protestant preachers, whether of the Scottish establishment or of the legion English sects, are in an altogether different category, since where amongst them there is any 'ordination', no claim is made to indelibility of character, as in the Church. 'Once a priest, always a priest'. The suggestion that the place of the clergy should be taken by women argues either an ignorance or a contemptuous ignoring of an Apostolic injunction governing the universal practice of the Church, and in consequence will not carry the slightest weight with any reverent-minded person.

As for your correspondent's characterisation of the 'arguments of the Archbishop as to comfort, consolation, &c.' as 'nonsense', I submit that the whole tone of his letter shows that in this, as in other points, he is obviously talking of matters wholly outside the sphere of his experience, and that this fact also vitiates his concluding aspersions on the Church of England and her clergy.

Yours, &c.,

M.E.M. Donaldson
Croydon

———

THE PRIMARY DUTY

SIR – I am quite sure that many of your clerical readers agree rather with 'Emeritus' in today's issue of your paper than with some of the bishops. It is very questionable whether the latter fully understand the whole position, as they are scarcely in any degree whatever in touch with the people.

A parochial clergyman knows fully what are his pastoral duties, just as well as the bishops do; and if it is clear that that is our primary duty we shall most of us stick to it, whoever disagrees with it, unless, of course, the State calls us up, and then we shall follow out Article 38, to which even every bishop has subscribed, 'It is lawful for Christian men, at the commandment of the magistrates to wear weapons, and serve in the war.' 'Christian men' of course includes bishops, priests and deacons.

The Speaker said a few months ago that if a German force landed on our shore we needed every man to be ready. What could the clergy do in such an emergency if their sons and others were abroad? There is not sufficient defence in walking about with a pastoral staff.

I am, personally, very disappointed at the attitude of the bishops. Let them point out manfully that a clergyman is not doing wrong in shouldering a rifle, and being ready to defend his home, his country, his King, the honour of his wife and daughters and other men's wives and daughters, but also state plainly that whilst getting ready by learning to shoot, learning ambulance work, &c., they should comfort their flocks, visit the dying, preach the Word. 'Put your trust in God, and keep your powder dry.'

I venture to say most of us are far more helped in this matter by my Lord of Carlisle than all the other statements by archbishops and bishops put together.

Yours truly,

A Vicar
Lancashire

———

A MATTER FOR THE BISHOPS

SIR – Your correspondents who are in favour of the clergy entering the Army as combatants appear to omit the following considerations:

1. That an ever-increasing number of chaplains are urgently needed for the Army and Navy.
2. That the work of the Church at home must be carried on and extended, and that the more strenuous part of it requires young and strong men.
3. That if there is grave danger (by depleting the ranks of young medical men) of injuring the future physical health of the nation, how infinitely more important is it to provide for its spiritual needs.

4. It is a question for the ecclesiastical authorities alone to decide. The clergy owe the same allegiance to their superiors as do the officers of the Army to theirs. Could one imagine our archbishops attempting to incite men to defy Lord Kitchener or Sir John French?

Yours obediently,

Churchyard

———

JOURNEY TO DEATH

Terrible Stories of Armenian Sufferings
A Million Lives

SIR – Herewith I send you some further details of the cruelties practised in the massacres and wholesale deportations of Christians by the Turkish Government in Asia Minor. These come via the United States, from sources on which the fullest reliance may be placed – foreigners engaged in hospital work in a town where several streams of deported Armenians converged at a stage, in their journey to death.

Names and other indications that might lead to identification are necessarily suppressed, to avoid danger to persons referred to, including a high Turkish official who tried to alleviate the cruelties, but was not permitted to do so.

Lest I should trespass too far upon your space I omit a careful estimate by a competent authority of the total destruction of life. Taking the total numbers of Armenians in Turkey at about two million, he thinks nearly a million have perished.

Faithfully yours,

Bryce

————

I

After a time large numbers of the exiles at X were allowed to find shelter in the town, where they rented houses, and for a time were better off. But they were not allowed to rest in quiet. Suddenly the order would come from the police that all were to leave for Y, and the whole number who were in the town, perhaps five thousand, would be driven (and I mean literally driven under the lash) into the streets with all their goods, and be rushed to the encampment. There, perhaps, a hundred wagons would be ready, and five hundred people find places and be sent off. The rest were then left to stay in the encampment or bribe their way back to the town again and re-rent their houses until another alarm and driving forth. Every such onslaught meant several mejids of expense for every family for transporting their goods and bedding to and fro, and this in addition to the bribes paid to the police for the privilege of going back to the town. Such bakshishes had to be paid to the police for every favour asked, from mejids (about 3s 2d) to liras (slightly less than £1 sterling). No one could go to present a petition to the Governor without bribing the police first.

In the encampment the police would come along in the morning and order all tents in a certain section taken down, saying they were to start for Y, and this order would be enforced instantly with scourge and club. The terror of the people from the reports they had of that journey 'beyond', of pillage, murder, outrage, stealing of girls, and starvation, was such that they were always ready to purchase a few days' respite if they had any money to do it with. No train or wagon is ready, so when enough money is brought out the people are graciously allowed to put up their tents again twenty feet away from their former site. The sick, the aged, none were respected. The people have described to me the terror of that constantly recurring order, 'Down with the tents', with the whip behind it.

Robbery, Outrage, Murder

The Armenians of Z sent here were forced to come by wagon. The Circassians of the region knew of it, and followed after and robbed them and shot one girl. Gendarmes were sent out after the Circassians, and only took their turn in the stripping of the party. Another party sent in the same way was attacked at night by Circassians, and one of the men shot through the thigh, a horrible wound. He died here in the hospital a few days later.

Hardly anything makes me so hot as the thought of the soldiers' families. The men, the fathers, brothers, sons, husband, are serving in the Turkish army as loyally as any, and their families, their children, with wives and sisters, are driven off in this inhuman manner. Soldiers' families are also said to be exempt from deportation, but in countless cases they are swept away with the rest. The wife must put in a special petition claiming her relationship. This petition has to be paid for, for she cannot write Osmanli. Oh, I wish you could see the abominable cruelty of the treatment and the diabolical ingenuity of the ways to strip them of all their money before having them die. For that is where it will surely end for all of those people unless some means of stopping it is soon found.

I must add a report from K, from which I have tonight received what I have every reason to believe to be an accurate account. Some two or three weeks ago about two hundred of the chief Armenians were imprisoned, then taken at night in wagons, thirty or forty at a time, to the river bank and there killed. Eighteen of the employees of the railway and the director of the bank were among these. I had this on good authority then, and it is confirmed now. Within this past week all the Armenian men, whether Gregorian, Protestant or Catholic, have been taken, stripped to shirt and drawers, tied together and taken away and heard of no more.

The women and girls have been distributed to the Turkish villages, and Turks coming and looking over the girls and choosing what they wanted. I could give you the name of one of the wealthiest men in K whose wife and three daughters were taken away before his eyes and who went crazy. Three hundred boys were circumcised. The name of the railway official was told me who saw a hundred of these done and reported it.

————

II

It is terrible to refuse asylum to girls whom we know to be in danger. Yesterday an unusually pretty and refined young girl of fifteen was brought to us by her parents; she had been pursued all the way from W by an Army officer, but they had been able to elude him, and the police as well. Our hospital is too public to shelter her, and we are still looking for a place for her. Most of the people in town are scared to do anything at all, foreigners included, but we don't propose to show the white feather, and are only waiting for certain official persons to return from X, where they went a few days ago in order to get larger liberties for Red Cross activities. At present our hospital has taken in all the soldiers and refugees that it can, and we are seeing sick refugees in the clinic all day long.

Today I counted twenty-one women and children in one of our waiting rooms mostly lying on the floor from sheer exhaustion, one child moribund, two others nearly so, and half the rest of the group quite likely to die in a few days if they are allowed to remain where they are in the camp. Many of the villagers are mountaineers, and lying out in the hot dusty plain by day and exposed to the cold of night they quickly succumb. Today I took a little girl into the hospital who had been perfectly well until four days ago, when everything was stolen from the mother and she had no place to lay her except on the ground, so that she quickly got up a dysentery and died a few hours after admission to the ward. The family were respectable Protestant people from V. Hardly had the little girl died and the sheets been changed than another child, this time a boy, was put into the same bed; his leg had been cut off by a railroad car, apparently there was nobody to take care of him. We found that the mother had been forcibly separated from her children further back on the road.

Their Only Crime

In that same ward lies a young girl who has recently had her leg amputated for the same accident, and who today was crying and screaming because some friends had told her that her parents had suddenly been deported to X without having been given a chance to see her. It is all horrible, horrible – no mere description can adequately portray the awful suffering of these unfortunate people whose only crime is that they are Armenian.

These people are being deliberately done to death at a sufficiently slow pace to allow their oppressors the opportunity of choosing out such of their women and their goods as they care for and getting all their money away from them before they die. Dr and Mrs A. went through the massacres of 1894 and 1896, and they and Miss B and I have been through two revolutions, one massacre and two wars since then: but we all agree that we have never seen anything like this. Another outrageous side of it is that many of the fathers and brothers of these women and children are in the army fighting the country's battles: such was the case of the dying child that was brought to the clinic this afternoon, and another who will probably be in the same condition soon.

———

16 December 1915

FOUND ON THE BATTLEFIELD

SIR – Two pencil and wash drawings have come into my possession, as follows:

1. A Lady; the drawing having the following written on it: 'A Sketch for Arthur's dug-out. – L.H.'
2. A Child; the drawing bears the signature: 'Doris Hocknell'.

Both are enclosed in celluloid facings.

Being desirous of returning them to the owner I should be pleased if you will assist me by making it known through the medium of your paper.

I am, &c.,
W.J. Norburn, Major, AOD
Havre

———

30 December 1915

ORGANISATION OF THE COUNTRY'S RESOURCES

Utilising Every Class

SIR – We are an indifferently organised nation. The war has plainly told us that. We have prospered by individual effort, and big men with a genius for seeing along the road of progress have carried with them the smaller men unaccustomed to think out problems by themselves. But a nation organised in wartime to bring out the best its population can produce must be infinitely stronger than one which does little to concentrate the whole energies of its people upon the work of production.

How many have asked themselves the question recently, 'What can I do to serve best the Empire at the most critical stage of its history?' The number of people unable to enrol themselves in the fighting forces, or to take part in the work of munition making, is extremely high. Whether it is one hundred thousand, half a million, or a million, it must cause deep concern to the Government if the energies of this mass are misapplied, or are not applied to uses which build up the national wealth. In the last few weeks the public have frequently been told how important it is that production at home should be increased, and now that the Army strength has been raised to four million men the economic problem of keeping the nation's trade going at high pressure is rendered more difficult of solution than ever it was. So acute must it become that the nation is bound to look for new sources of labour supply, and to expect production from classes which hitherto have not entered the fields of industry.

Men and Women

There is at this moment a great opportunity for rendering a national service of inestimable value by sound, practical men in thinking out and developing a scheme for utilising large classes of the people at present producing nothing. The bulk of these would be delighted to accept a suggestion as to how they could help the country. Men of leisure over military age or unfit for military service, professional men whose careers have been temporarily checked owing to the war, and employees in industries which the war has injured form a considerable portion of the population, and anyone who is aware of the efforts made by these classes to obtain some useful war work knows how wide a demand there is for any scheme under which they could be employed.

The war has brought home to us that we had been too hesitating in the employment of women in many industries. Institutions which before the war scorned the idea that women could do the work then performed by men have availed themselves of women's help, and speak in the highest terms of the performance of their duties, of punctuality, good temper and steady application to their tasks. In factories of all descriptions women have taken the place of men who have patriotically gone to the colours. If it be true that there are hundreds of thousands of women earning honourable wages today who had never sought employment before the war, it is clear the nation must be the richer for their services. It may be a labour problem will be created after the war, for, these women, having entered fields of enterprise for which they have proved their fitness, will not readily give up their employment. But that is a matter for after-war settlement. The point is that a great army of women is, in the time of the country's need, helping in a marvellous way to keep industry going, and what they are doing ought to prompt an enormous number of their sisters who are doing nothing for the country to come out and assist for the national good.

How to Use Them

The question is how can these men and women be helped to devote their energies for the welfare of the country. There must be countless ways for their profitable employment. The most attractive, of course, is munition-making or the manufacture of equipment for the troops, for everyone so engaged rightly appreciates that each article made goes directly to the defeat of the Allies' enemies. But so does the production of every necessary article made at home. This is a war in which money plays a part as vital as that of men. Anyone devoting money and labour to the production of food in this country is preventing the importation of a corresponding amount, and keeps money at home which would otherwise go abroad. The balance sheet of the amateur poultry farmer, even if it shows an adverse balance, is a patriotic document during the war, and anyone who has cut his flower garden in half that he may grow vegetables may be satisfied he is doing a service by raising food. Similarly, every week employed in maxing articles which, if not required at home, may be exported and bring money into the country, is given to the nation's cause.

The people who could be employed, and – there is no doubt about it – who wish to be employed, if there was some organisation to direct their energies into appropriate channels, are waiting a lead. Cannot some method be devised for utilising the services of the mass of people who, if not idle, are not doing all they can to promote the national welfare, and whose inactivity, owing to the weakness of national organisation, constitutes a national waste? Would it not be possible for some practical men to consider how all the available material in men and women could be passed into spheres of usefulness, where each person, while profiting by the output of honourable labour, will get an even greater return in the knowledge that he or she has done some part in helping the country to win the war, and to prepare for the struggle for industrial supremacy when peace comes?

A Central Bureau

If a number of public-spirited ladies and gentlemen could be got together to organise and control a central bureau in London, with branches throughout the country, to arrange that the unemployed energies of the people should be directed to the work of production, the country would conduct the final phase of the war with a greatly increased force. Many people believe they have qualifications which would make them useful, but they do not know how or where to offer their services. There are others who do not know they possess qualifications, but they are ready and anxious to be instructed, and if they could be informed how they could do something for their country they would render willing service.

The central bureau could inquire what lines of employment would be useful, collect the personnel for such employment, and develop schemes for the employment of all possible workers outside the existing lines of public service. What the labour exchanges do for skilled and unskilled labour, the central bureau, or by whatever title it was known, could do for the large class which is not doing, but is anxious to do, all it can for the good of the country. This body might have a small beginning, but it would work for a class which is as patriotic as any in the country, and if its labours were well directed there are possibilities of effecting great and far-reaching benefits for the Empire.

Suggestions Wanted

Suggestions for the carrying out of such a scheme would be helpful to those who are considering it, and would be welcomed. While any hastily formed ideas might prejudice the chances of success, the question of utilising the fullest possible strength of the nation to finish the war is of such importance that it brooks no delay. A plan to bring to the country's aid the majority of the non-productive elements of the population does not necessarily mean the setting-up of a new and costly organisation throughout the kingdom There is already in being the machinery for assisting in the carrying out of such a scheme as is suggested in this column, and the advantage of employing that machinery might be obtained if it was made evident that a well-considered and useful scheme was framed.

The success of Lord Derby's plan of recruiting was in a large measure due to the tremendous amount of work put into the organisation by the political party agents throughout the country. They brought to bear a wide experience and a sound knowledge of men and matters, and at a time when the tide of recruiting seemed about to ebb they helped forward the flood with a rush. The party agents and the local committees in every ward of every borough and every polling district of every county are in touch with every section of the community. They are patriotic men, and would assuredly give their valuable assistance to any plan which would bring out the whole of the country's resources at a time when every citizen of the Empire should lend a hand to win the war. Properly organised, there could be no more efficient source for the collection and distribution of personnel than the united organisations of the political parties of the State.

I may also point out that the County Territorial Associations contain many of the most influential men in the counties. At this day it is unnecessary to refer to the untiring work these gentlemen have ungrudgingly given for the public good. Many of them – practically all of military age – are now serving with the Army, but there are left a number of older men of great influence and capacity who would be readily available, and could be used with the best advantage for the purposes of the scheme. The paid staffs of the associations have already so much to do that they are unable to attend to more, but a small special staff under each official secretary of associations could render useful service. The cost would not be heavy, and as the scheme would work for the benefit of the nation the financing of it would be a charge on the public funds.

I am, your obedient servant,

Middle Class

———

4 January 1916

'WAITING FOR THE OPPORTUNITY'

SIR – The very able letter signed 'Middle Class' appearing in your issue of yesterday's date raises a matter of vital national importance. There are thousands of men in Greater London alone over military age with long and practical experience of commercial and business life, like myself, who are only waiting for the opportunity to take up work at once and help in this time of need for as long as our services are required. Surely a Central Bureau could be quickly formed which would do for the large and willing class who are longing to help what the labour exchanges are doing for skilled and unskilled labour.

I am, &c.,
A Willing One
Sutton

PUBLIC SCHOOL BOYS' OFFER

SIR – May I suggest a means of employing a considerable number of young Britons? I am a public school boy. Every term I see some of my schoolfellows leave to take commissions in the Navy and Army, and our old boys' roll of honour is, alas! very long. Those of us who are too young to serve the King would be proud to render any useful service to the country. We have games for two hours each afternoon which we would cheerfully give up.

I suppose it would not a practical thing to suggest that lathes for the manufacture of munitions should be put up in our workshops and gymnasium, because it would not be profitable to run machinery for only two hours each day. But there are many things we could do, and if there are 50,000 public school boys in the kingdom ready to give up their spare time for at least two hours each day, it is surely a national waste not to employ us.

At the end of three months the output of boys who collectively worked 100,000 hours a day would be prodigious. I am sure our masters would help the cause, and would instruct us in any work allotted by the Government. The Germans, we hear, compel their boys to work. Why not accept the free offer of public school boys to work for Britain?

Your obedient servant,

Upper Middle

NATION'S EAGERNESS

SIR – With reference to the admirable letter, signed 'Middle Class', appearing in today's *Daily Telegraph*, I am sure the writer's views will be supported by a large section of the community of would-be workers. Let some enterprising individuals of the energy and courage of Lord Derby but embark on this scheme of organising the formation of local bureaux where voluntary workers can apply for some form of personal service; there is no doubt that the idea would be taken up heart and soul by the nation, and all would feel they were doing their bit.

I am, dear Sir, yours truly,

Mary S. Edwards
Chine Hall, Spa Road, Boscombe, Hants

SERVICE FOR ALL

SIR – Most people will agree with 'Middle Class' as to the necessity of organising the resources of the nation, and it appears to me that this can readily be accomplished. Lord Derby has with the help of information from the National Register organised the men of military age for military service. It is rumoured that in one direction the voluntary response has not been satisfactory, and that some measure of compulsion is now to be adopted – so far so good.

It is agreed, however, that if we are to carry this war on to a successful conclusion we must have not only more men for the fighting lines, but more munition workers, and that fresh sources of supply of labour must be tapped if the vital industries of the nation are to be kept going. It is admitted that female labour must be more and more extensively used; but we must not overlook the fact that there are many men of the leisured classes at the present time absolutely unoccupied.

Why should not Lord Derby's scheme be applied to men over military age with a view to civil employment in the interests of the Empire? Let them be canvassed preferably by men who have been canvassed, attested and passed to the Army Reserve. Let those who are willing to respond to the call of their country register at the labour exchanges. If the response is not satisfactory, let them be compelled to register. There is no need to devise some more select agency. The labour exchange is just now as honourable a place for those over military age to use as is the recruiting office for those of military age. Class distinctions are anathema at this time of the Empire's peril.

After registration each man who was not in useful employment would be sent where he would be of most use and most needed. For instance, the retired Civil servant would be sent back to the Service to release those eligible for the Army. Those who are not capable of taking posts of responsibility would be drafted as unskilled labourers to munition works or to those trades whose continuance is of vital importance to the country.

When it is urged that it would be incongruous for such men to work as unskilled labourers and to receive the pay of an unskilled labourer, it is overlooked that at the present time many a former leader of industry is serving in the ranks of the Army and receiving the pay of a private. Again, if and when many businessmen are called up in their groups under the Derby scheme, their businesses will smash and, if married, their homes will be broken up, for there will be no employer to supplement their Army pay. In comparison with such sacrifices, that of the leisured man would fade into insignificance.

We hear a great deal of the young unmarried slacker, but let us not overlook those equally blameworthy – those over military age who are doing nothing when every man should be doing something to help in this time of need.

Yours, &c.,

Gilbert B. Soddy
Eastbourne

MEN AND MACHINES IDLE

SIR – Our Government has for a long time been expending enormous sums of money in building new factories in and around London for the purpose of manufacturing munitions of war. After these factories are built, they have to be fitted out with machinery and power, all these machines have to be brought into the country at a very big expense, and the men who our Government asks to go to London and work these machines are men physically fit for the Army. My suggestion is that none of these new factories are required.

There is now and always has been a very large number of machines, a large amount of space already built, and enormous power to work the machines standing idle in this country, and in the different towns where these machines, space and power are situated, there is a number of men who are too old to fight who could work a lathe, and they are too old to leave their homes and go to London and work in the Government factories. These men could if they were given the opportunity not only work a lathe, but they could teach the boys and women to work them in a very few days, hence we could get the whole of our munitions manufactured in our country towns, thereby releasing many thousands of eligible men from the huge factories in London and other places.

It seems a great pity that so much of the country's money should be wasted in building factories when there is no need. And, again, there are thousands of idle fingers as your correspondent suggests only too willing and eager to do necessary work for their country, if they only had the opportunity. To give work to these idle fingers I would like to suggest that not only munitions of war are required, but there is work that others could do if they could see and know what was required. To give them this opportunity there should be a sample sent of anything and everything that is required by the Government into each town and exhibited in some large room or hall, so that the inhabitants who are willing could go and see what was required, and in a moment see if they could help in its manufacture.

I feel confident that everything that is needed could be made in this way, and all willing and idle fingers could be quickly set at work if our Government could be induced to try a scheme of this kind.

Yours truly,

A Country Engineer
Tunbridge Wells

————

THE NATIONAL REGISTER

SIR – The letter of 'Middle Class' in your issue of today emphasises the paramount duty of the Government to utilise immediately the services of the large number of ineligible men, and also women, to bring this war to a successful issue.

Up to the present I have seen no authoritative a statistics of the National Registration, and I venture to say action should be taken on the results of this census. Doubtless a large sum of money was spent on this, as well as on Lord Derby's scheme, and it would be wasteful to allow such an expenditure of capital without securing the fullest return.

A responsible committee should be formed, either by the Government, or outside the range of politics, and make the national registration forms the basis of their work. With the co-operation of newspaper proprietors the public would soon become acquainted with the fact there was a central bureau (with branches) to whom to apply for work of any kind during the progress of the war.

The real work of decentralising into areas of cities or counties and corresponding with likely applicants, &c., could easily be carried out if office expenses were defrayed out of public funds.

I am, Sir, your obedient servant,

Organiser
Bristol

———

5 January 1916

LINES OF ATTACK

SIR – Having read with great interest the admirable letter of 'Middle Class' which appeared in your issue of 30 December, will you allow me to suggest that many of your correspondents seem to have missed the main points of his idea?

Surely his argument was this: There is still a vast amount of energy in this country not being used directly or indirectly against the enemy; let us then put our heads together and decide (1) into what channels that unused energy may be directed; (2) the best means of collecting and directing that energy in the channels chosen.

For example, all methods of increasing the food production of this county would economically strengthen us; I take it that practical suggestions to this end are invited from experienced and competent authorities. There are thousands of men and women who might be led on this line of attack. Are there not other lines along which we may harass, and thwart and harm and weaken our enemy?

Every ounce that we as a nation can put into the weight of our blows should be used now. Is not that what 'Middle Class' means? We want to be shown and instructed in all possible weapons of attack. The personnel is waiting.

I am, Sir your obedient servant,

Basil Hood
88 St James's Street, S.W.

———

THE STEREOTYPED REPLY

SIR – I have read with much interest the letter from 'Middle Class' on the organisation of the country's resources. There are doubtless other cases similar to my own. At the outbreak of war I was practising as a consulting engineer in London. At the end of September 1914, I finished up the work I had on hand, and then went to the War Office to see if I could get anything to do in the motor transport service or in any direction where my knowledge of engineering could be used.

I was requested to put in my application in writing, which I did promptly. About a week afterwards I had an acknowledgment of this letter from the secretary, thanking me for the offer of services, and advising me to take no further steps until hearing from him. I had no further communication, I am forty-six years of age, and in my application to the War Office I mentioned that I had already seen service in Rhodesia during the rebellion, when I was in the artillery.

I next tried the anti-aircraft service, but was informed at the Admiralty that the lists were full. I then joined the Special Constabulary. With the advent of the Ministry of Munitions I applied there by letter, but was switched on to the Board of Trade, who wrote pointing out that there were no higher appointments open, but that the great need for the moment was for skilled workers, but that if I cared to put my name down on the engineers' war service register I could do so. Having been through all the shops in one of the largest shipbuilding and engineering firms on the Clyde, and also having done a good bit of pioneering work in the Colonies, I have kept myself proficient in the use of tools, so that I thought myself pretty useful in this way, and at once put my name down. Still nothing doing!

The only little consolation I can obtain is from the thought that I have produced a lot of chicken flesh, eggs and vegetables, and am keeping thirty-two laying hens and pullets, but I cannot help feeling that I could be doing greater things in taking an engineer's part in what has been termed an 'engineers' war'.

I am, Sir, yours obediently,

C.E.
Sunningdale

————

6 January 1916

ORGANISATION OF THE COUNTRY'S RESOURCES

Wanted, a Businessman

SIR – Now that the recruiting campaign has come to a close I quite agree with you that it is high time that far weightier matters should be earnestly considered. It cannot be denied that carrying on the war is the most gigantic business that the world has ever witnessed.

To carry on this stupendous business successfully the whole of the organisation must be centred in the brain of one man who has had years of training and subsequent experience in organising and carrying on an extensive manufacturing business.

The most serious point is the utter want of complete harmonious organisation of the country for the purposes of the war. The organisation falls naturally into four great classes, as follows:

1. We have, say, 4,000,000 men in the Army and Navy, who must be provided with everything necessary to keep them up to the fullest possible state of efficiency.
2. To provide for all their wants an enormous army of men and women is required.
3. To maintain these providers another section of our people must work to produce enough of the necessaries of life to maintain the whole population.
4. Beyond these requirements we have to provide the sinews of war. This can only be done by keeping up and increasing our exports to such an extent as will pay for our imports, the cost of which, however, is very largely reduced by sums due to this country for interest on foreign investments, shipping freights and other matters; in short, every effort must be made to pay for imports otherwise than with gold.

Failure in one of these classes spells failure of the whole business. These four great classes would each be sub-divided, but not too minutely. Ever since the beginning of the war the nation has been fed with the ridiculous swaggering nonsense that our silver bullets would win the victory for us. Certainly, the Government has been firing off the silver bullets fast enough, but the victory is still far out of sight. It is time that we abandoned the silly silver bullet craze, and realised the fact that victory depends on hard work, governed and regulated by the very best organising talent we possess.

Energy Running to Waste

At present all is confusion; energy runs wild because such vast numbers of the population, being anxious to assist, get no direction of any kind. All this energy ought not to be allowed to run to waste for a single day. To every man, woman and child between the ages of eight and eighty should be allotted such work as he or she could do. Such apportionment of work must be made with discernment of the individual capability; no round pegs in square holes.

At first sight the foregoing suggestion appears to be utterly impossible of realisation, but, fortunately, we have great organisations which readily lend themselves to adaptation to the object in view. The first, and by far the greatest, difficulty is to find the man, with great knowledge and brain power, in whom the whole scheme of organisation must be centred; there must be no divided authority at the very top. A head having been found, he gives to each member of the Cabinet a department of the organisation work. Each of the Ministers will employ his particular department in carrying out the duties assigned to him, but each must report to the head. The Ministers will further delegate to county councils, corporations and councils (urban and district) such further detail work as they can undertake.

All these bodies are responsible to their superior department, which in turn is responsible to the head. The necessity for having an autocratic head is that the working of the organisation must be perfectly harmonious; in a multitude of counsellors there may be wisdom, but very seldom perfect harmony. As a matter of course, the head would receive many suggestions from the Ministers, hut he must be absolute judge of the value of such suggestions in the matter of harmonious working in the great machine.

Such an autocratic head as I contemplate would not be a great speech maker; he would have known for years that 'great talkers are little doers'.

Yours faithfully,

Walter East

AN EMPLOYMENT CANVASS

SIR – The letter signed 'Middle Class' comes at a most opportune moment.

I wrote on Tuesday to the Local Government Board, and pointed out that when the local tribunals began to hear appeals for exemption by employers, it would greatly ease the situation if the employers had access to extracts from information furnished under the National Registration from women of no occupation who professed their willingness to undertake work of any kind.

Such women would readily respond to appeals for their services, endorsed as they might be by the local tribunal, and feel they were doing a most direct, personal and patriotic duty in thus facilitating the release of men for the Army. The requests for service would come largely from local employers, and be directed to local residents, and would reach a class of women that would never see ordinary advertisements for workers because it does not look for work.

As regards the main question, why not a Parliamentary Employment Committee, working through the local Parliamentary associations and the local tribunal? This method of utilising the local agents, as your correspondent points out, has produced splendid results; the organisation is intact, it has the workers, and is thoroughly experienced. And why not an employment canvass to ascertain exactly the feasibility of utilising the services of each of the women who declared willingness to serve? Such a canvass working in close unison with the local tribunals should have the very best results.

As a member of an important London local tribunal, I should like to see all tribunals assume some responsibility for replacing labour recruited for active Army service, thus satisfying as far as may be both the needs of commerce and the necessity of filling up the ranks.

Yours,

T. Owen Jacobsen, JP
Newton House, Paternoster Square, E.C.

WORK FOR WOMEN

SIR – Your Civil Service correspondent's interesting communication requires one addition, or, perhaps, correction. He says that no serious attempt has been made to bring in for war service the huge mass of the educated middle-class women of England.

He should have added that the War Office, through the Head Mistresses' Association, are offering women of this type holding the equivalent of honours degrees at Oxford and Cambridge, and of the highest intelligence, 25s weekly for a forty-eight-hour week, with an obligation to work unlimited overtime at 9d an hour. It may be possible to justify the wage on the ground that people anxious to help are willing to accept it. It is not possible to justify the length of hours per week wherein labour is required.

My company, with a wide and long experience of women clerks and typists, are satisfied that only a woman of exceptional physique, of whom, alas, there are but few, can work continuously at office duties for more than thirty-nine hours a week. Any attempt to extend this working time, if it lasts for more than a week or two, leads to tired and inefficient work, and a heavy sick list.

If women are to take the place of first- and second-division clerks they should be paid not less than half of the salary of the men they are replacing, and the hours should be carefully adjusted.

Yours,

Secretary

———

THE ANTI-AIRCRAFT CORPS

SIR – I have read with considerable interest the letter in the issue of the 29th signed 'Middle Class', and I think my own experience will show how very discouraging the authorities can be, however anxious one may be to render some little assistance. Being upwards of fifty years of age I many months since offered my services to the Anti-Aircraft Corps, and was told that I should be called upon as further stations were opened. From time to time I have called and have written, with no result, but a few weeks since, I received a summons to report myself, when my services were not only accepted, but I was told the station I should be sent to as soon as it was ready.

On this I resigned from the Special Constabulary, giving my reason that I had joined the Anti-Aircraft Corps. Yesterday I received a notification from the corps that as the defences of London had been taken over by the military authorities, my services would not now be required. This I contend is hardly what one would call business.

I am, Sir, your obedient servant,

A.E. White
Hampton Wick

---

7 January 1916

ENGINEER'S EXPERIENCES

SIR – Having read with much appreciative interest the letter signed 'Middle Class', I would like to place before your readers my experiences as an engineer, having a matured knowledge of most of the natural sciences, a practical experience of over thirty years in engineering work generally, and a speaking acquaintance with at least six different languages, and, perhaps what is most to the purpose, a knowledge of organisation, having at one time occupied a high position in the Government service as inspector of mines and explosives. Since the war started I have made several applications for work, as follows:

I applied through the Labour Bureau and was directed to the Board of Trade department connected with engineers at Queen Anne's Gate, who referred me to the chief inspector, Woolwich Arsenal. Having filled in two forms, in duplicate, giving a detailed account of my education and experience throughout my life, I waited patiently and am still waiting. I also was recommended by a high official at Scotland Yard to apply to the Censor's Department for work, as I had a good knowledge of German, French, Dutch, Flemish, Spanish, Russian and Turkish. After waiting several months and also filling in three forms, and giving two first-class references, I was finally informed that my services would not be required. I then made an application to the Committee for the Relief of Professional Classes in Wartime, not for charity, but for work, and all the satisfaction I got was to be referred to one of the most prominent institutions of engineers, of which I was not only a late member of council, but practically a foundation member!

On the other side of the picture I have given all my time and energy, free of pay, to Government service, 1) as a special constable, having the privilege of paying £5 for my uniform; 2) in assisting the Criminal Investigation Department in, of course, an amateur capacity, in trapping spies and undesirables generally, and succeeded, so I was informed, in doing very efficient work for the department. I also offered my services, free of all charge, expenses only to be paid, to the Red Cross and St John Ambulance, but, not having sufficient money to pay the expenses of living, &c., I was obliged to refuse all offers. Finally, I enlisted in the Sportsman's Battalion, age thirty-nine and 'a bit', no questions being asked as to the amount of 'the bit', which should have been twenty years more! Anyway, now I have the satisfaction of being able to comply with His Majesty's request to wear the armlet, when it is finally delivered to me.

This is the story which I hear repeated on all sides by brother engineers of the greatest ability and experience. Surely nothing but sheer want of proper organisation in the

Government departments, save always the Admiralty, which has never been 'too late', could warrant such 'blinking incapacity', as Tommy would call it.

I am, Sir, yours, &c.,

Special Constable

————

1 January 1916

A NEW YEAR'S WISH

SIR – At the turn of the year, the second December that has witnessed the continuation of the lurid drama enacted by the international players on the chessboard of the world's politics, permit me to offer you the greetings of the new year, with the fervent prayer that it may prove to you and us all a far happier one than that of 1915.

This is no conventional wish: there is something specially opportune in rendering to you these good wishes, shared, I am convinced, by your large circle of readers; for, frightful as have been in more ways than one the attendant miseries of the holocaust 'war', your journal has ever been prompt to the fore in the humane effort to alleviate the brutal effects of this world struggle, to soften the wounds that have been so mercilessly inflicted in this premeditated attempt to set back by several degrees the hands of the dial and to arrest that phase of the world's progress termed 'civilisation'.

In other words, by the splendid manner in which you have intuitively grasped and strikingly expressed the needs of the hour, by your timely and eloquent advocacy on behalf of the wretched victims of the various forms of suffering entailed by warfare's insane methods, by the princely and magnanimous response you have always been able to evoke in aid of suffering humanity in this country and in the countries of our Allies, you have earned a debt of gratitude from those who witness in silence, as well as from those who are directly benefited by the working of the powerful means at your command for influencing public opinion – a debt that can never be expressed in words, and one that is bound to grow with the months of conflict that are still before us.

I am sure you will agree with me that there can be no more solemn aspiration at the present hour than the prayer that the day may not be far distant when the maxim 'Peace on earth, goodwill towards men' may prove not merely a splendid text for this time of the year, but a living reality for all times and all seasons.

Yours obediently,

Hermann Gollancz

3 January 1916

A DERBY RECRUIT'S COMPLAINT

SIR – Yesterday most of the daily and evening newspapers published a request to all those men who had been attested under Lord Derby's scheme to wear the armlet, and thus show a proof to one's fellow countrymen of one's response to the call. I am one of those who are entitled to wear this much-talked-of armlet, but I am unable to show this proof of my response to the call for the simple reason that I cannot get possession of one, and write, in view of the King's request, in the hope that my grievance, which is no doubt borne by countless others, may soon be rectified.

To put my case briefly, I was medically examined, approved and attested at Wimbledon as far back as 20 November. The following week I made application for an armlet, and was told that they had not arrived. The following week I was told a similar tale, and that they would be posted to those entitled to them by a certain day. Needless to say, the day arrived without the armlet. My next application was a few days before Christmas, when I was informed that they would only be issued to those up to the age of twenty-six until after Christmas.

When I saw the King's request yesterday I thought surely I should get one at last, and made a special journey for the purpose last night. This time I was told they were only issuing them to married men up to the age of twenty-eight, and that I should most likely be able to have one next week. Surely this is an unusual procedure, and cannot be said to be due to the lack in the number of armlets, and it would not be out of place, therefore, to ask those who are responsible for some explanation on the matter with a view to those like myself being able to carry out the wishes of our King.

Yours truly,

A Would-be Armleteer
Wimbledon Park, S.W.

---

6 January 1916

LORD DERBY'S SCHEME

Medical Students

SIR – It has been brought to our notice that local tribunals are to inquire into the reasons why certain individuals have not joined His Majesty's Forces. We would like to point out the difficulties with which we, as medical students, have had to contend. In October, 1915, the beginning of the university year, we were all informed by the Cambridge medical authorities that it was our sole duty to continue our medical studies. In addition, a letter from Lord Kitchener remained posted up in the medical schools authorising those instructions, and urging medical students already having taken combatant commissions to return to their studies, and that they would be discharged on application. Then came a week of crisis. Lord Derby, in his urgent need for men, pointed out that the duty of junior medical students was to take combatant commissions. While on the one hand Lord Derby claimed us, on the other, the majority of medical authorities, amongst whom were Professor Clifford Allbutt, Sir Frederick Treves and Dr Shipley, pointed out the shortsightedness of this policy. After listening to these various contradictory statements, our duty was not very apparent. The difficulty has not yet been cleared up, as can be seen from the following example. A medical student, in the same plight as ourselves, only yesterday applied for enlightenment on this subject from an officer of high rank in His Majesty's Forces, and was told to 'sit tight'. What are we to do?

We are trying to make ourselves useful by working as dressers at the 1st Eastern General Hospital, and we wear the Royal Army Medical Corps' collar badges, but we are not officially recognised by the War Office. We are doing Government work which is not officially recognised by the Government. We are unable to continue work as dressers during term time as our superior officers refuse to accept us on the grounds that our medical studies are of more vital importance to the country. However, we carry on ambulance work in the Cambridge University Officers Training Corps (Medical Unit).

Are we justified in 'sitting tight', and what answer shall we make to the local tribunals?

Yours faithfully,
Three Medical Students
Queens' College, Cambridge

7 January 1916

LIGHTS ON VEHICLES

Cartage Contractors' Difficulty

SIR – May I, as president of the London Master Carmen's Association, appeal to you to allow me space in your paper to ventilate what is a great injustice to owners of horse-drawn vehicles, namely, the strict enforcement of the new order issued on 30 September last compelling owners to place a red rear light on every vehicle. We all agree that the order is a necessary one in the present abnormally darkened streets, and immediately it was issued the trade ordered approximately 15,000 lamps for London alone, but, owing largely to lamp manufacturers being engaged on munition work, it was found impossible to obtain even a quarter of the number required.

Transport must be done, and to carry out the law, if lamps cannot be obtained, conveyances must not be worked after dark, or, alternatively, the owners of vehicles are to be summoned for non-compliance. It is obvious that no blame can be attached to the owner of the vehicle if it is impossible for him to obtain the lamp, and, whilst some magistrates are imposing a light fine, owners in most cases having to pay the costs, there are occasions when heavy fines are imposed.

I therefore feel that if the Home Office desires the order to be strictly carried out, it should under the circumstances see that the vehicle owners are able to obtain the wherewithal to do so, and I venture to suggest that if those summonses continue it may be necessary for the owners of vehicles to withdraw their conveyances from the streets at dusk, to the serious disadvantage of those relying on the transport trade.

I am, Sir, yours truly,

(Signed) G.A. Dutfield
17 Water Lane, Great Tower Street, E.C.

————

19 January 1916

BOOKS FOR THE ARMIES

SIR – An organisation has been formed with the title of 'The Fighting Forces Book Council'. It is important to know that while this has the approval of the War Office, Colonial Office and Board of Education, and of the High Commissioners of the Dominions beyond the Seas, this organisation is intended to supplement, and not in any way to overlap, the existing organisations such as the Camps Library, which is the recognised collecting and distributing depot for the books sent through the medium of the General Post Office, the Red Cross and St John Ambulance War Library, which supplies the hospitals and the Young Men's Christian Association. Through the machinery of these various organisations, large quantities of books are being regularly supplied to the Forces on active service, naval and military hospitals, and convalescent camps, both at home and abroad. The work done by these organisations is, however (mainly, if not entirely), that of distributing agents for the books generously supplied by the public, and sent by them through the Post Office or otherwise. These books are naturally of a miscellaneous kind, and consist preponderantly of light fiction, and the enormous numbers of books issued to the troops (about a hundred thousand weekly) make any systematic selection or classification impossible.

It has, however, been found that books of a more solid kind are largely asked for by an immense number of educated men now in the military service of the Empire, who find themselves cut off from the studies in which they were engaged, and which they are still anxious to pursue.

The objectives of 'The Fighting Forces Book Council' will therefore be to try to meet this need and at the same time to assist the existing organisations in every possible way. It proposes to:

1. Raise funds for providing reading matter of the kind indicated above for His Majesty's Forces at home and abroad, including the wounded and convalescent and the British prisoners of war.
2. Procure, by purchase or gift, boosts of this kind in sufficient quantities, and arrange for their distribution through the Camps Library to the various organisations and corps.
3. Draw up lists of such books required by, or suitable for, various types of men.

The Fighting Forces Book Council is pursuing these objects, not only in concert with the above-named organisations, but also with the support of the Incorporated Society of Authors, the Library Association, the Publishers' Association of Great Britain and Ireland, the National Home Reading Union and other like bodies. The council consists of representatives of almost every branch of letters and every side of public life.

An appeal is now therefore made for funds to carry on its work, and we feel sure that we need add nothing to commend such an appeal to the public.

Contributions forwarded to us or to the London County and Westminster Bank, Law Courts Branch, W.C., will be duly acknowledged.

We are, Sir, your obedient servants,

E.W. Ward, Chairman, Executive Council
I. Gollancz, Hon. Treasurer
Hon. Secretary
Alfred Perceval Graves, Hon. Literary Director
Seymour House, 17 Waterloo Place, S.W.

---

5 February 1916

LINGUISTS AS CENSORS

SIR – With reference to your publication of the official notice regarding the censorship of letters and the apparent dearth of qualified linguists, permit me to state my experience. In response to my application I was invited to call for an official interview, and was given letters in French, German, Spanish, Italian and Portuguese, all of which I translated orally to the satisfaction of the examiner; but when I was informed that the salary would be only 30s–35s weekly I said I could not entertain the offer, as it would not be possible to live decently on such remuneration. I add that I was at an English public school, that I subsequently spent nearly three years in France, and that I have had a long commercial experience.

I am, yours faithfully,

X

—————

9 February 1916

WOMEN'S WAR SERVICE

A Scheme Worthy of Help

SIR – In your issues of yesterday and of today's date there have appeared two articles on 'Women as Welders' and 'How Posts are Found' respectively. The intelligent appreciation shown in these articles of a work as useful and fascinating as its inception has been unobtrusive, is bound to attract widespread attention. May we therefore beg of you still one more valuable service? We want through your columns to ask for public help, as well as interest, in order to extend our possibilities of usefulness in these directions.

Every woman selected for her fitness and trained to expert usefulness is, in our opinion, worth a soldier at the front: she only can liberate the 'starred' man, and therefore selection and training are our watchwords. Success of the sort which alone justifies our appeal has been so far ours all along the line; namely, the highly satisfactory quality of the work which our students turn out, and the fact that aircraft and munition factories swallow them up as fast as we can supply them. Incidental expenses must be met, and we want scholarships to help the women, the most suitable of whom cannot themselves bear the expenses of training and maintenance meanwhile. Will the more serious minded of your readers come forward and help us? We are aware that such work makes but little appeal through glamour or sentiment, and it has been organised by a Suffrage society!

May we, in this latter connection, point out that in pre-war times, in those far-off 'happy days when we were so miserable', we formed and perfected an organisation on strictly constitutional lines in order to get the vote for ourselves, but in the face of the national need it was our pride and privilege to turn over that organisation whole-heartedly and unreservedly to the national service. We believe it was no mean gift. Our women's hospitals in France and Serbia, our Belgian brothers and sisters here, can answer for us. Will you help us to carry on now this invaluable work for our sisters at home?

The Hon. Mrs Spencer Graves will receive very gratefully donations addressed to her at 59 Victoria Street, and further inquiries at the same address will be welcomed by the Women's Service Bureau.

Yours faithfully,

(Signed)
Frances Balfour (President)
Annie Cowdray
B.M. Graves (Hon. Treasurer)
Gertrude Kinnell
Edith Lyttleton
Women's Service Bureau, 58 Victoria Street, Westminster, S.W.

CHURCHES AND THE WAR

A Layman's Suggestions

SIR – Apropos the letter in Monday's *Daily Telegraph*, regarding a proposed autumn work of 'Repentance and Hope', might I be allowed the great privilege of ventilating through your powerful columns a few thoughts or suggestions of a mere and very insignificant layman?

I would venture most respectfully to suggest for the consideration of those most competent to judge of the matter – that is, the leaders or heads of the religious bodies in this country, and perhaps elsewhere:

1. That, if feasible, arrangements be made to organise effectually, and carry out, a work of real and genuine prayer, accompanied by some voluntary penance – otherwise self-denial – amongst all classes and ages and both sexes as an act of reparation to our Creator and Master for our shortcomings and neglect of Him and His teaching in the past.

2. That such work should, if possible, be particularly devoted to one special week, to include the day of the Patron Saint of England – St George.

3. That this offering of prayer and voluntary penance be addressed to England's Saint asking his intercession with the Almighty to succour and aid not only those in this country, but also those in all our dependencies, to overcome and muzzle for the future the ferocious dragon of uncivilised militarism.

4. That in order to make this effort really effective, and to bring religion to the masses, open-air services be held during the special week in as many suitable places as possible, and at convenient and promising times during the day, with early morning services in all the churches.

5. That special early morning and evening services be arranged and held in all our churches on next St George's Day.

Such a work of earnest prayer and reparation would surely bring down upon us and our arms in this righteous war for civilisation the blessing of Heaven, and doubtless procure for us in the not remote future that permanent, honourable and lasting peace which the whole world is looking for.

Apologising for trespassing upon your kindness and courtesy, I am, Sir, yours truly,

M

----

21 February 1916

A MISUNDERSTOOD WORD

Attesting and Starring

SIR – I notice in the *Daily Telegraph* that it is stated that there appears to be considerable difficulty among men of an eligible age to understand the difference between 'attesting' and 'enlisting'. May I suggest, from a very considerable number of applications made to me for advice from men of all agricultural occupations, that the real difficulty is that they do not understand the meaning of the word 'attest', or 'test' as it is pronounced in this county generally, and that they confuse it with a medical test which they do not consider at all necessary if they are persons who are entitled to be starred, or exempt, from service; and it is curious, but absolutely true, that it is almost impossible to make many of them believe that they must be attested before they can be starred.

Let me now give one instance out of very many: A miller desired to ask my advice how he could be 'starred', and on being told that he must go to Lincoln and be 'attested', and

then appeal, he said, 'Tested, tested! Cannot I go to Dr —',
mentioning the nearest local medical man, 'and be tested?' I
could multiply examples, but will not ask more space in your
valuable paper, and only conclude by expressing great fear
lest this confusion of ideas should lead to a lot of trouble and
some hardships.

Yours faithfully,

Heneage
Hainton Hall, Lincoln

———

8 March 1916

'TOO OLD AT FORTY'

Sir – Your leader in today's *Daily Telegraph* on National
Organisation certainly touches the spot. I am one of
thousands who came over from the Colonies to offer my
services during the war, only to be put off from every
department I have applied to. In one instance I am told I am
too old, being forty, but I am sound in every way, and good
for another twenty years' hard work.

I have employed and controlled over a thousand men,
mechanics and labourers, and earn a very large salary in the
Colony I come from. Yet my services are refused even when
offered free. Surely there must be work for everyone who

volunteers and is willing to throw up everything and return to the Mother Country to assist.

Yours faithfully,

Colonial Engineer

———

9 March 1916

BANKERS' POINT OF VIEW

SIR – In my capacity of manager of a very considerable provincial banking business extending over a wide area, I have recently found opportunity to ascertain the views of many of my investing customers regarding the subject of the suggested issue of premium bonds; and, except in two or three instances, they have expressed themselves as being not only favourable to the proposal, but as eagerly awaiting the chance to subscribe to such an issue, if it be made.

The only opponents are parties who have 'conscientious objections' to anything which they can conceive to savour of gambling, being quite unable to perceive that, as your correspondents point out, strictly, this element does not enter into the question at all. One, in particular, most strongly denounces the 'iniquity' of the scheme; and yet, having a most confident belief in the outcome of the war and in the future of the Empire, is making large investments at present low prices, with a view to the rich reward which he confidently hopes to reap by-and-by!

From the bankers' point of view, such an issue is, manifestly, not to be desired, as it would entail an enormous depletion of the deposit moneys now held by them at interest rates ranging from 2½ to 3½ per cent; and which, despite the huge sums I already raised on War Loans, still, for all practical purposes, remain intact. It seems, on the face, to be fairly obvious that when the small depositors – whose money constitutes the great bulk of that held by bankers – can obtain an English Government security, not subject to market depreciation, yielding so good a rate as three per cent. fixed, and offering at least a sporting chance of sudden fortune, a very large proportion of this money is bound to be withdrawn from bankers' hands.

Most of those with whom I have discussed the question hold that such an issue would be morally beneficial, inasmuch as it would serve to divert into a channel useful to the interests of the State that sporting instinct in English people which restrictive legislation can never eradicate; and also because those who subscribed to it would be saving money, instead of impoverishing themselves and their dependents by betting, speculation, or whatever other form they choose for their 'little flutter'.

There can be no doubt that a great deterrent to investment in previous War Loans has been the well-founded dread of reduced yield, and consequent depreciation of capital, arising from the incidence of an increasing income tax; but let the proposed premium bonds be issued – free of tax – and the prospects of success may be considered illimitable.

Yours faithfully,

An Old Bank Manager

———

THE SMALL INVESTOR

SIR – Your correspondent 'Finance', in his courageous and reasoned contribution on Saturday, and your city editor and 'A City Merchant' today, have surely made out a good case for premium bonds. If, as your city editor suggests, such an issue might not appeal to the big investor, at all costs let us have a premium bond issue as part of the next War Loan.

Your contributors all refer to the desirability of making the issue attractive to the small investor, but they appear to stop short at the £100 investor. Is not one of the problems of the moment the attachment of the surplus earnings of munition and other wage-earners whose earnings are much in excess of the normal? If this is achieved, the further result is attained that expenditure is reduced, especially upon luxuries.

Exhortation to economy will serve little purpose, but provide a tempting investment that will appeal to the industrial communities of Lancashire and Yorkshire, the Midlands and the north, and that result will be attained. It is, I suppose, recognised that the subscriptions in small amounts both to the War Loan and for Exchequer bonds has been, and is, disappointing. Why? Not because the money is not available, but because simplicity of method has been lacking, and because procedure has been hampered by formalities and delays.

If our Government will issue premium bonds in multiples of £1, and will issue them through every bank and Post Office in the kingdom, direct over the counter in exchange for gold, silver or Treasury notes, without any formality whatever, that is, sell them like postage stamps, they will be surprised at the results. Interest might be at 2½ per cent, payable by means of perforated coupons attached, with a premium bonus of 1 or 1½ in addition. As regards this section of the issue it should remain open for the duration of the war, and a heavy weekly inflow would be realised.

Your correspondents anticipate opposition. Have we not had rather a surfeit of opposition, and has not the conduct of the war in various directions been hampered by those who even yet are unwilling to recognise that the times are not normal, and that therefore methods need be abnormal? Let Mr McKenna take a strong line on this question, and opposition will speedily fade.

A Banker

EXPERIENCE OF FRANCE

SIR – I am very glad to see you have opened your columns to those who are bringing forward the question of the issue of premium bonds. I am confident that not only a large sum of money could be raised by this means, but also that the social and ethical effect would be far-reaching and of great value.

I have lived a good deal in France, and have discussed with various Frenchmen the methods whereby they have succeeded in getting the idea into the heads of the great bulk of the working men and women that saving is a normal and ordinary part of civilised existence. One can indeed go so far as to say that among large classes of French it is considered bad form not to have something put by. I have been told that premium bonds have been one of the main causes of this state of things.

With us, if a working man saves £5 or £10 what can he do with it? Practically all that is open to him is either the savings bank, where it lies at a rate of interest which produces him a negligible sum, or a building society, where security is not by any means always of the first order. Whereas in a premium bond you get the best possible security for capital in a very realisable asset, a small sure rate of interest plus the chance of making a very good profit; in fact, just the very qualities trustees look for in a trustee investment.

Premium bonds would appeal to the sporting instincts of the working man, and this in a way essentially different to a lottery. For in a lottery you most probably lose what you put in, and in a premium bond you cannot do so. I have great hopes they would so what is so wanted now, viz., induce men who are making more money than ever before to put some by instead of indulging in unaccustomed luxuries. This would be of great good to themselves, and also would create here a *petit rentier* class, who are the strength and backbone of France. To bring this about I hope that there would not only be the large prizes your correspondent speaks of today, to tempt the richer investor, but also a very considerable number of smaller prizes, say £3 or £5, to improve the chances of the small investor making a profit.

I am, &c.,

Observer

————

WORKMEN'S INVENTIONS

SIR – The great activity in munition factories and other controlled works has brought to light the general lack of knowledge regarding the rights of employees with regard to inventions which they may make.

The actual law upon this matter is that, if a workman makes an invention, that invention belongs entirely to him, 'Even though the article may be made in the employer's time, and with his tools and materials.' The quotation is from the judgment of Mr Justice Farwell in the case of Marshall and Naylor's patent, which is the ruling case on this subject. If, however, the employer instructs a man to work out an idea, then the invention is the property of the master, and the workman has no right to any recognition for simply working out the improvements explained to him.

The general impression amongst the employers, however, appears to be that an invention made by a workman in the course of his work is the master's property, and if, as is sometimes the case, the workman is given some small (usually inadequate) recognition of his zeal, this is looked upon as generosity on the master's part. In some cases the employer even goes so far as to patent the invention in his own name, which is, of course, illegal.

Now, as patent agent to the members of most of the large trade union societies (numbering nearly a quarter of a million skilled artisans), I am aware of many cases in which workmen have made valuable improvements which have resulted in material profit. Usually the inventor is complimented upon his ingenuity, but when he asks what recompense he is to receive he is told that he has only done his duty. Should the workman have the temerity to patent his invention, which he has a perfect right to do, the employer is indignant, and I am aware of one case in which the workman was actually dismissed, and in another case revocation of the patent is threatened.

In some large works awards committees have been set up to settle the recognition to be given to a workman for any invention he may make, but it is exceedingly doubtful if the award ever reaches the value of the improvement; for, of course, the workman has little choice but to take what is offered him, and usually these awards committees are very slow, and often no award is granted at all, even though the employer continues to use the employee's invention and profit by it.

Inventions in the workshops of great utility to manufacturers have been practically stifled by the methods referred to, and there are hundreds of workmen in this land who could bear out this statement from either their own or their fellows' experiences. The very best way to induce the skilled men to make inventions and improvements to benefit the nation and assist us in our struggle for commercial supremacy is to convince them that they will be adequately and fairly rewarded.

Yours faithfully,

Geo. H. Rayner
5 Chancery Lane, E.C.

———

14 *March 1916*

HUTS FOR THE ARMY

SIR – A few weeks ago I addressed a letter to the press asking for money, or gifts in kind, for the YMCA, and particularly alluded to February as the YMCA month.

People have already sent donations from one penny upwards to cheques, crossed London County and Westminster Bank, for whole huts named after places or fallen heroes of the war. Twenty huts are, roughly, my total up to now, but many, many more are wanted with this rapidly increasing Navy and Army, and the upkeep always has to be considered, for the expenses of the YMCA are about £500 a day. The Navy has responded nobly with donations from the canteens, and with a few more gifts I hope to put up one, or, perhaps, two huts, called 'The Navy', likewise 'The Nurse', also 'The Farmer'.

The donors have been most ingenious, from collecting pence at a mothers' meeting to ½d fine for a spot on the tablecloth, 10s, or a 1d a grumble, which raised 10s and caused much amusement. Whist drives, concerts, sewing parties, cake competitions (the cakes being given to the hospitals afterwards), baby shows, bazaars, rummage sales, farm kitchen concerts, lectures, and sales of rings or curios have also been held.

Could everyone who reads this letter not find some means by which to help this scheme? The YMCA is the fighting men's club. It is unsectarian: it is open to everyone in the King's uniform; and millions of letters to the homes of the Empire would never have been written but for the free gift of the paper and envelope bearing the well-known red triangle.

Faithfully yours,

E. Alec-Tweedie
30 York Terrace, Harley Street, W.

25 March 1916

'WHERE AM I IN THE WAR?'

SIR – For many years the press at this season has granted me space to invite recruits in their days of health for personal service in the cause of the sick. A season of war is not all loss, for already it has enabled hundreds of thousands to shed self and devote their energies mainly to war work. In this way many have substituted direct for vicarious service for the sick, and attained their ideal. I welcome these escapes from the depths of solitude represented by the inner feelings and aspirations previously hidden away in the hearts of a multitude of men and women in London and other great centres.

But there yet remains a majority of that multitude who in these days of laborious toil and laborious pleasure-seeking may be conscious of an inner thirst for the humanising influences which flow to those who devote a measure of their time to wholesome work or to brighten the lives of their neighbours. My heart goes out in sympathy with these secret aspirations now stirring in human hearts, and I hope once more to put this majority on the road where they can shed existence for life.

In many cases an apprehension of the health value of self-destruction would bring permanent relief. In such cases discipline is the real physic when deliberately applied with personal energy, for then it can convert discontented or relatively valueless members of society into human beings of the first rank. This type includes the people who still give themselves up to amusement. If they could only realise the outer darkness in which they must find themselves when the war is over, and the prolonged misery it must prove to be, unless they apply the remedy which is open to them today, they would avoid the risk of being out of touch with the realities of life and of degenerating into mere human wreckage.

Who can plumb the depths of degradation touched by a British man or woman (and I know some such) who, to the neglect of their plain duties, are obsessed with the pursuit of every 'anti' craze, and insistently devote their remaining sympathies and resources to pampering the Germans in our midst who are prisoners or interned? It has not been possible so far to apply the drastic treatment such people need and deserve, but the wholesome stiffening up of public opinion, to the exclusion of false sentiment, amid the awakening of patriotic apprehension are hastening the time when the remedy will be forthcoming and applied.

The season of Lent might usefully be availed of by every one of us asking himself, 'Where am I in the war?' Our country needs every one of us, and we elders who have to remain at home often find the work we are called upon to do greater than ever before. Is it not amazing that there should be slackers and human sloths of both sexes still strutting in our midst? Have such people no brains, or love of country, or even self-respect? They cannot even live in any true meaning of the word, for they merely exist in fact, whilst every day such brain power as their parents gave them must be diminished of to make room for the fibrous tissue the n. use of their faculties continuously develops. I would venture to beg all men and women who have both brains and ideas, but refuse to use them for fear they may have to work harder, to awaken to a full realisation of their spiritual being, and give it full play by embracing higher ideals and entering upon a truer life. This latter type might do most valuable service in many ways, without any risk of over-strain from the excitement of war work. They could, indeed, make themselves of supreme use to their country at the present crisis. This way lies blessedness and the joy of living.

If it were only possible to widen the vision and excite the apprehension of every man and woman amongst us, who is yet without his or her portion in the business of the death-struggle in which our nation and Empire are engaged, can we believe that each one of them who asks, 'Where am I in the war?' will rest content to continue a human sloth, will not awaken to the seriousness of the life which surrounds them, and acquire the will to enter into it? Even the older people, through prayer and intercession, can renew their youth. Then they will set their minds and those of their acquaintance to think out what the country will need after the war, and how they can help to make a real Merrie England of the best.

Herein lies the impetus which should arouse and urge forward every man and woman amongst us capable of real thought. Than each one of them will see to it that they will prepare themselves and their neighbours for the great changes and immense upheaval which must follow the war,

271

ent it is concluded there may be throughout

added wisdom in support of higher ideals. If

action can be aroused, it will secure the

of the nation through the people, and will yield

should make England and Empire the embodiment

of the best and most ennobling system of government of which the world is capable.

I am, Sir, yours faithfully,

Henry C. Burdett
The Lodge, 13 Porchester Square, W.

---

30 August 1916

MORALITY AND THE STAGE

Sib H. Smith-Dorrien's Appeal

SIR – I can no longer refrain from invoking your help in an appeal to certain theatrical managers to endeavour to raise the tone of performances they prepare for the public, especially for the younger members of our fighting professions.

I am convinced that our gallant sailors and soldiers themselves would be the first to admit that if they were given their choice, they would prefer a performance which, whilst cheerful and inspiring, appealed to the best side of their patriotic natures, and not exhibitions of scantily dressed girls and songs of doubtful character.

The whole nation's heart is at last set on winning this great war, and an important factor undoubtedly is the cleanliness of mind and the nobility of purpose of our heroes on sea and land, and it seems entirely unnecessary, and certainly wrong, to put into their heads demoralising thoughts, such as they must obtain from many performances now appearing on the stage.

Yours truly,

H.S. Smith-Dorrien, General
Cell Farm, Old Windsor

———

10 October 1916

NATION'S MAN-POWER

Firemen and Tribunal Conditions

SIR – The recent circular issued by the president of the Local Government Board to the local and appeal tribunals refers to previous instructions whereby the granting of exemptions should be conditional that some form of voluntary national service should be undertaken, and it provides that it may be unwise to ask a man who is already engaged upon national service to undertake additional service in another branch or branches.

The executive of the National Fire Brigades Union specially called the attention of the Government to the obvious hardships incurred upon fire brigade men who are not classed in a certified occupation, whereby additional duties were imposed upon them by local tribunals.

It is not generally known to the public that the duties of the fire brigades have been multiplied since the outbreak of war, extra voluntary air-raid duties, extra hours needed for the training of recruits, extra risks incurred by munition factories working at high pressure, the protection of numerous naval and military works, such as depots, hospitals, camps, &c. All the foregoing must receive attention, no matter how much the fire brigade are reduced by the loss of trained and competent staffs. It is for the national welfare and for the sake of humanity that protection from fire must be afforded. The service will therefore welcome the removal of the extra compulsory duties, and it is hoped that the suggestion of the president of the Local Government Board will be made retrospective by the local and appeal tribunals, seeing that the season when fires are generally more prevalent is close at hand.

I am, Sir, yours faithfully,

W.G. Webster, Acting Secretary, National Fire Brigades' Union
22 Northumberland Avenue

IRELAND AND THE ARMY

'Dangers' of Compulsion
Mr O'Brien's Suggestion

SIR – The abortive partition proposals did more than the Dublin severities to recreate a disaffection which had practically ceased to exist. It passes belief that any Ministers in their senses can now be meditating the still worse blunder of military compulsion, which would make that disaffection all but universal and irreconcilable, and yet the incredible seems to be happening. While reasoning has still any chance of a hearing, give me leave to submit a few practical considerations, before the last voice for reconciliation between the two countries is stifled.

1. No Irish Nationalist ever promised peace in Ireland except on condition of Home Rule. The feebleness – not to say double dealing – of two English Ministries has left us in a chaos in which Home Rule is neither granted nor rejected – neither dead nor alive. And this torment of Tantalus has been rendered unbearable by Mr Lloyd George's success in procuring from a pensioned Irish party their consent to what Mr Sexton (surely no mad Sinn Féiner) has described as the vivisection of our country.

Irish at the Front

2. Nevertheless, even a disappointed Ireland has not only contributed to the Army 100,000 Nationalists resident in Ireland, but 150,000 no less ardent Nationalists in Great

Britain, and at least 150,000 more from Canada, Australia, New Zealand and South Africa – a considerably larger contingent than even Canada, with twice Ireland's population, and five times her wealth, has been able to put in the field. Sir Edward Carson has not been able to furnish more than 25,000 of his Covenanters, but because they have been concentrated in one purely Covenanting Division, and have been allowed to fight as a unit in the same field, with a gallantry of which all their countrymen are proud, England rings with gratitude to the Ulster Division, while Nationalist soldiers, at least fifteen times more numerous, and nobody will deny equally gallant, are unfortunately scattered incoherently among dozens of divisions, and, far from earning England's undying thanks, read little except bitter reproaches and insults to their race. Those who would have Englishmen believe that Irish soldiers in Picardy and Macedonia are indignant that compulsory service is not enforced against their kindred at home know so little of these soldiers' inmost hearts that the effect upon their moral of conscription in Ireland is, on the contrary, one of the gravest of the dangers that ought to give wise statesmanship pause. And those who are horrified at the wastage of the Irish divisions being made up by Englishmen strangely forget that the wastage of dozens of London, Liverpool, Manchester and Tyneside regiments is very largely made good by Irish Nationalists.

3. What would be the practical effect on England's fighting strength of a campaign to enforce Conscription in Ireland? I am quite aware of the bearing a candid answer may

have on the future prospects of Home Rule. That consideration has quite certainly its weight with the English and Ulster politicians, who are stirring up the clamour for the coercion of Ireland. It is nonetheless of as much importance to England as to Ireland that those who have struggled hardest for peace and goodwill should fearlessly declare that the enforcement of Compulsory Service would mean the most horrible campaign for the reconquest of Ireland England has ever had to undertake. No Nationalist member of Parliament of any section could let a Compulsory Bill pass through the House of Commons without a resistance taking every possible form of violent and world-resounding protests, and without devoting their lives to an uncompromising campaign to make oppression bitter for the Government and Parliament of England. It is not even certain that they would be without an unexpected amount of aid from English Liberalism of the old strain, laid under enchantment though it has been of late by the wizardry of Mr Lloyd George, and from the Labour Party, not a dozen of whom could hope to be re-elected without Irish Nationalist votes.

A Desperate Struggle

And the Parliamentary resistance would be only the preliminary to a struggle from parish to parish in Ireland, in which England could not count upon support of any kind, moral or material, except her own bayonets and machine guns. For obvious reasons, I abstain from gratifying the enemy by particularising the nature of that resistance. Mr

Duke is doubtless in possession of information sufficiently enlightening on the subject. That part of it which would be carried on with firearms before recruits could be laid hands upon would be the smallest part of the difficulty of coping with a universal system of passive resistance, such as all who have endeavoured to coerce Ireland in the past can picture to themselves, and such as no army can effectively conquer. There are those who would console you with the suggestion that the Irishman is a dangerous man to run away from. Ask your German enemies whether an Irishman is not sometimes a dangerous man to stand up to.

All is lost as between the two countries if it be held a bad turn to England to make her realise that in such a struggle she would be dealing with a race as solid and as desperate as the people of France, Belgium or Serbia in their own fight for life. And for what is this deadly enmity of a race to be challenged? To add a body of at the utmost 60,000 valid recruits to an army of five or six millions, and to do it by maintaining in Ireland an army as numerous at the least, with the certainty that whatever Irish recruits might be kidnapped by the press-gang would return from the war a trained army of infuriated enemies of England. What would be the effect upon the Allies, upon the United States and upon the weakening Central Empires, of this bitter and, in the nature of things, never-ending war upon the Irish race, surely no man in the Cabinet can be so infatuated as to speculate without horror.

Nor let it be imagined that Ireland's resistance would be daunted by the fate of the Home Rule Act, should English prejudice grow unhappily once more uncontrollable. What

Cardinal Logue said of partition can be repeated with redoubled emphasis of conscription, that all Irish Nationalists worth their salt would 'prefer to go out into the wilderness for fifty years more' rather than submit to the one or to the other.

For the recruiting difficulty, as for all other Irish difficulties, there can be only one remedy that will not be worse than the disease. It is to call together the responsible heads of all Irish political parties, interests and denominations to devise a new basis of national self-government for their country, and to have their recommendations ratified by Parliament, subject to any modifications an Imperial conference may hereafter find to be equitable. One would suppose it is the most obvious of counsels, but it has never yet been tried, and if it is to be effective for recruiting purposes or for any others, it must be tried promptly and before the war is over.

Your obedient servant,

William O'Brien
Mallow

———

18 October 1916

'FOR ALL WHO HAVE FALLEN'

SIR – The mothers of England will owe you a debt of the deepest gratitude if through the agency of your columns you can open up the question of distinctive badges for the fallen, and obtain for us a coveted decoration in memory of our beloved dead. As the mother of an only son who volunteered in the first month of the war at the age of eighteen, and laid down his life at Ypres only seven months later, I thank you with all my heart for allowing your columns to voice this burning question.

Yours gratefully,

One of the Mothers
Wembley

———

2 *January 1917*

WOUNDED OFFICERS

SIR – For some time past I have received appeals regarding a hardship which officers sent home wounded or suffering from illnesses contracted on foreign service are encountering on their arrival in this country, from what I feel sure is mainly due to insufficient forethought or organisation. As the House is not sitting, may I be allowed to allude to it in your columns? It is the practice of despatching these officers to hospitals far away from their respective homes, where they have no friends, and where, owing to the increasing difficulties of travel, visits from any friends must necessarily be few and far between. It is not as if these officers were all cot patients. Many are convalescent, some are perfectly fit, and only waiting to have minor operations, and are not undergoing any medical or surgical treatment at all.

Only recently a specific case was brought to my notice where some dozen officers, practically all of whom belonged to the south, were rushed up to the north of England, on the ground that 'all the London hospitals were full'. We all know that this is not the case; some of the London hospitals are for the most part empty. Of course, it may be suggested that these men could be transferred to hospitals near their respective homes, but this is a three weeks' business, and in the meantime many of these men are kept without leave, and only have permission to leave the hospitals for a few hours each day. One would have thought that both in the interests of the State and of the men themselves it would be better to send them home, where most of them have hardly been for more than ten days since the start of the war, to benefit as much as possible by home comforts.

May I suggest that in the case of officers who are sufficiently well to move about:

1. They should be allowed to go to the hospitals nearest to their homes, should they so desire it, subject, of course, to there being room at the time.
2. Transfers should be granted forthwith.
3. Pending such transfers being arranged for, officers should be given leave.
4. Commandants of hospitals should, subject to mutual agreement, have power to transfer at once by notifying

headquarters, but without the need for the long waiting period.

Many thousands of officers are affected by this matter, and I do therefore think that it is worth the attention of the authorities.

Yours faithfully,

Warwick Brookes, MP for Mile End
London

———

22 January 1917

SAFETY OF MUNITION WORK

SIR – We all recognise regretfully the necessity for tens of thousands of people working daily on munitions and handling in various ways high explosives. We also know that stringent precautions are taken in order to secure comparative safety and immunity from accident. The cause of the recent explosion is unknown, and may have been unpreventable, but as one who has connection with a number of such workers I am writing to urge, in the interests of the men, women, girls and youths who are thus employed, that the whole question of their safety should receive fresh and prompt attention. When we realise the loss of human life and property caused by the explosion on Friday last, and the amount of suffering caused thereby, we are compelled to ask whether the punishment meted out by certain magistrates to persons convicted of carelessness in such employment is adequate to the seriousness of the offence. Fines for such ought in the interest of the community to be abolished and imprisonment substituted in every case. The trade union leaders have done much in this matter, but so long as magistrates show such excessive leniency their efforts will be in vain. Possibly the law may have to be strengthened before the difficulty raised can be met.

One other point. Is it necessary that such dangerous work should be carried on in crowded and poor districts? Usually the cottage property all round the works is crowded to excess; and is of such a nature that the slightest shock causes collapse, with disastrous results. Is it too much to ask that this kind of work should be removed from such centres? Not to do so is to court the maximum of loss and suffering when any disaster occurs. In the midst of the many matters requiring attention I trust that in the interests of the working classes, to whom the whole country owes so much for their loyalty and magnificent spirit in the midst of this titanic struggle, this matter may receive that careful attention, at the hands of the Government, which it certainly deserves.

Sincerely yours,

J.E.
Bishopscourt, Chelmsford

15 June 1917

THE BAN ON RACING

Mr E.S. Tattersall's Views

SIR – I read with much interest the articles which you published on Monday under the titles 'The Ban on Racing' and 'Racing and Breeding: Danger to British Stock'. In the latter you say that owners and breeders have reason to hope that before the end of this month sanction will have been given to resume racing at Newmarket, and you most truly add, 'Such a decision is urgently needed to prevent a catastrophe to horse breeding from which it might never entirely recover.' You have not exaggerated the urgent necessity for the speedy resumption of racing, with, no unreasonable and unpractical restrictions. Everyone interested in horse breeding agrees with you. Having been hon. secretary of the Hunters' Improvement Society, in its first two years – 1886 and 1887 – when the thoroughbred stallion shows commenced, and being now hon. treasurer of that society, as well as of the Thoroughbred Breeders' Association, may I be permitted to say a few words endorsing your prophecy? Most breeders and owners and trainers of thoroughbred horses and people interested in horse breeding are my friends, and the outlook for them is gloomy in the extreme. Lord Curzon, in his recent speech in the House of Lords, to which I listened with interest, admitted that 'in its wonderful thoroughbred stock the country possessed a national asset of almost incalculable value', and said that 'the Government had no desire to exercise a disturbing influence upon the position of that asset'. That asset, however, depends on being reasonably and publicly tested, and on an outlet being provided for it in the shape of a market within the United Kingdom, as well as for export. The average amount for which we ourselves sold horses for export in 1911, 1912 and 1913 was over £123,000, and many horses were sold publicly and privately besides to go out of the country. The horses we sold for export in 1914 made £30,000 only.

It seems calculated to make us the laughing stock of the world to throw away such a valuable, useful and necessary product for an almost infinitesimal and negligible saving of oats. The lives of many men depend on horses. It will be remembered that at the beginning of the war 150,000 useful horses were quickly available in the United Kingdom, and since then 250,000 more, owing almost entirely to private enterprise in horse breeding, which may be looked on as a gift to the State. In any case private breeders have saved the State much expense and trouble. Racing is to some extent an amusement, but it is one which results in a useful product. Without racing, and a substantial amount of it, we shall be unable to distinguish between soft, unreliable horses and stout, enduring ones. There should be sufficient racing to enable the public to make a proper selection of our thoroughbred stock. The limitation of racing to Newmarket only, where it was carried out on restricted lines and with no sign of beanfeasting this spring, was only just sufficient to keep the stream flowing. What should we think of a Government which forbade or seriously hampered the production of sugar or cotton in the countries best suited to grow them? In the United Kingdom, thanks to our climate, we have been able, and shall be able, if the facilities are granted which expert opinion with regard to horse breeding considers necessary, to breed horses which all countries of the world envy and are compelled to come to buy, and the quality of which permeates to some extent nearly every type of serviceable horse. It is a necessity for all foreigners to return frequently to England and Ireland to buy our stock.

It has already greatly cheered and amused our enemies to hear that racing is stopped here. They know well that racing is essential to test the merits of horses and prevent us breeding rubbish. So do our Allies. I have received messages lately from the leading owners and breeders in France, Italy, Russia and America urging us not to give up breeding and racing. Governor Stanley's speech at Louisville, made before the decision of the Kentucky Derby recently, is quoted in today's *Sportsman*, and he cannot speak too highly of the importance in wartime of the thoroughbred horse of Kentucky. In Germany and Austria racing continues; only in England has it been totally abandoned. It is, however, quite a mistake to suppose, as many do, that Irish breeders are able to keep up their studs if English racing is seriously crippled. The principal market for Irish breeders is in England, and many Irishmen practically depend for their living on the sales at Newmarket and Doncaster. One has recently written to me that he is ruined owing to the impossibility of selling his yearlings if the ban on racing continues. His case is one only of very many.

The seriousness of the outlook at Newmarket, which has been compared to a mining town with the mines shut down, has been described by the leading clergy and bankers of the town. A reason advanced lately by an anonymous breeder, that horses now being bred will not be available in the present war, and, therefore, it will do no harm to stop racing for two years, and run the now two-year-olds as four-year-olds, and so on, is impracticable. He does not seem to know that colts cannot be turned out for a year or two (certainly no one could afford to keep them in training idle), without injuring themselves and becoming useless. They would be undoubtedly operated on, and the continuity of horse breeding would be seriously affected. To insure this continuity racing is essential. The views of Professor Robert Wallace, given in today's *Sportsman* and *Sporting Life*, are stated, so lucidly and convincingly that they should be read by the authorities. Coming from a Professor of Agriculture and Rural Economy at Edinburgh, they compel attention. Horse breeding and agriculture are bound together, as Lord Middleton and Sir A.E. Pease have ably written. I think the resolution passed by the War Emergency Committee of the Royal Agricultural Society of England, has not had the prominence given to it that it deserved, and with their words I will conclude this lengthy letter.

'The Committee view with alarm the very serious effect the total stoppage of racing will have on horse breeding, and urge his Majesty's Government to remove the present drastic restrictions, which must inevitably have a far-reaching consequence by the wholesale reduction of colts necessary for stallions to maintain the production of the half-bred stock so urgently needed for military and national purposes.'

I remain, &c.,
E. Somerville Tattersall
Tattersall's, Knightsbridge, S.W.

23 July 1917

OLD WAR COMRADES

SIR – At the request of many who have served or are serving in our great Army, I desire through the medium of your valuable paper to give publicity to the wish felt by many of all ranks that, after having served together in this great war, we shall continue to keep in touch with one another after it has been fought to a finish. Between those of us who have spent long months and even years in the trenches, patiently waiting for the guns and shells which would place us on terms of equality with the enemy, there have grown up steady ties of affection and comradeship. Silently a general determination has developed that those who have endured much together should keep together to the end, always remembering those who have fallen by the way, and a resolve has been made that we should cement that spirit of comradeship for our mutual advantage and protection in the future. Sir, prompted by the highest motives, many thousands of soldiers desire this. By many it is thought that the best way of attaining this end would be to create throughout the land a similar organisation to the Old Comrades Association, one of the many bright spots of that little valiant army of the past. Examination shows, however, that while we might with advantage follow its excellent example and ideals, yet to deal with an Army of millions, the machinery would require enlarging.

Briefly, the idea is to establish a soldiers' association throughout the country and the Dominions. The motto might well be 'United We Stand', and I remember a worthy non-commissioned officer suggesting to me when discussing the idea before the Battle of Loos, why not call it 'Veterans of the Grand Army'. No better name could, I think, be suggested. Amongst the many objects of such an association would be the following:

1. To watch and safeguard the interest of all members of the Forces, and to take such steps as are necessary to protect them during and after demobilisation.
2. To promote undertakings for the disabled, using our individual and combined efforts to find employment for all discharged soldiers and sailors.
3. To help discharged soldiers and sailors to prepare their necessary papers, and to see that their pensions and allowances are in order.
4. To secure the welfare of the women and children left by those who have fallen.
5. To perpetuate in loving memory and affection the dead.
6. To promote amongst the rising generation the grand spirit of patriotism and devotion that is the characteristic of the Army of today.

To achieve these objects it would be necessary to have borough and county organisations throughout the country, with a grand central council. Parliament would be requested to grant a recognised uniform for authorised parades only, which parades could be held at intervals during the year or on a stated bank holiday. Membership would be free, with service as a qualification. Women should be admitted to the association to represent their husbands during their absence on service.

For the past two years these questions have been discussed in various forms, and the very definite desire is evident that when we drift back to civil life, whatever our vocations may be, we may still hold together as a living corporate body. It should be noted that the welfare of every trade or profession is safeguarded by some such organisation as is hereby suggested. There are a large number who desire to contribute annually toward the general funds to be used for this organisation, and for extending help when necessary, and I therefore ask you, as a token of your appreciation of our serving soldier, to give all the publicity possible to this suggestion. Through your valuable paper, I ask all officers, non-commissioned officers and men who are interested to communicate their views to the Hon. Secretary, VGA Association, 3 Central Buildings, Westminster, S.W.1. Those who have been connected with County or Regimental Associations in the past are particularly requested to communicate at once with the undersigned, so that at the earliest data possible a meeting of county representatives may be arranged to prepare and approve of the first bye-laws.

Yours, &c.,

J. Norton-Griffiths
3 Central Buildings, Westminster, S.W.1

———

29 October 1917

NAVAL AIR SERVICE 'COMFORTS'

SIR – May I ask for your very kind assistance in making known, through the medium of your widely read paper, this urgent appeal on behalf of the Royal Naval Air Service Comforts Fund (registered under the War Charities Act, 1916)? I venture to hope that the ever-generous public will again support this fund, which has distributed over 150,000 comforts during the last three years. Mufflers, cardigans, jerseys, mittens (dark blue or khaki coloured), socks (any colour), gramophones and games are urgently needed for the stations at home and abroad. Parcels should be marked RNAS Comforts Fund, and sent to Mrs Henry Balfour, Langley Lodge, Headington Hill, Oxford. Donations should be sent to the honorary treasurer, RNAS Comforts Fund, London City and Midland Bank, 129 New Bond Street, London. All will be most gratefully acknowledged.

Yours faithfully.

R.M. Sueter, Chairman and Honorary Treasurer,
RNAS Comforts Fund

30 October 1917

TOWARDS RECONSTRUCTION

SIR – We desire to appeal to all those who wish to see educated women take their proper share in the remaking of our country after the coming of peace to provide a fund which will enable them to fit themselves in time for the task which lies before them. Before the war it was plain to those who looked into the matter that a great deal of valuable work was lost to the nation, and much inefficient work was allowed to be a national hindrance, because parents and guardians had not sufficiently realised their duty in training the girls under their charge, and because these girls, when deprived of parental support, were without funds to pay for their own training. On the other hand, the war has shown what trained women can do. It is also showing daily that the supply of such women is not equal to the nation's need – a need which will increase rather than diminish when the great work of reconstruction begins in earnest. There is urgent necessity that educated women and girls should be trained now, not only for the time of peace, but to meet the present national demand. But training takes money as well as time, and too often, while time is short, money is not forthcoming.

The Central Bureau for the Employment of Women – at whose offices thousands of women are interviewed and advised year by year – established seven years ago a small fund which has done and is doing excellent service in helping educated women to meet the expenses of training, maintenance during training or, at times, outfit and business equipment. The fund is administered with the greatest care and forethought, but its usefulness is curtailed by lack of capital. The committee earnestly desire, therefore, to raise a sum of £10,000 immediately, to be devoted entirely to the preparation of educated women for useful and remunerative professions. Such a fund could but be a sound national investment, for what greater benefit can a nation reap than the health, happiness and efficiency of so many of its citizens? We need only add, in appealing to those who desire to see trained women take their proper place in the reconstruction of our country after the war, that the administrators of the existing fund, of which the Countess of Dudley is president, court the fullest inquiry into its financial stability, and that all donations may be addressed to the Countess of Dudley, at the offices of the Appeal Committee, Central Employment Bureau, 5 Princes Street, Cavendish Square, W.1

Yours,

Bryce
Selborne
Mary G. Spencer

29 November 1917

CO-ORDINATION OF ALLIES' WAR AIMS

Letter From Lord Lansdowne

SIR – We are now in the fourth year of the most dreadful war the world has known; a war in which, as Sir W. Robertson has lately informed us, 'the killed alone can be counted by the million, while the total number men engaged amounts to nearly twenty-four millions.' Ministers continue to tell us that they scan the horizon in vain for the prospect of a lasting peace. And without a lasting peace we all feel that the task we have set ourselves will remain unaccomplished.

But those who look forward with horror to the prolongation of the war, who believe that its wanton prolongation would be a crime, differing only in degree from that of the criminals who provoked it, may be excused if they scan the horizon anxiously in the hope of discovering there indications that the outlook may after all not be so hopeless as is supposed.

The obstacles are indeed formidable enough. We are constantly reminded of one of them. It is pointed out with force that, while we have not hesitated to put forward a general description of our war aims, the enemy have, though repeatedly challenged, refused to formulate theirs, and have limited themselves to vague and apparently insincere professions of readiness to negotiate with us.

The force of the argument cannot be gainsaid, but it is directed mainly to show that we are still far from agreement as to the territorial questions which must come up for settlement in connection with the terms of peace. These are, however, by no means the only question which will arise, and it is worth while to consider whether there are not others, also of first-rate importance, with regard to which the prospects of agreement are less remote.

Let me examine one or two of those. What are we fighting for? To beat the Germans? Certainly. But that is not an end in itself. We want to inflict signal defeat upon the Central Powers, not out of mere vindictiveness, but in the hope of saving the world from a recurrence of the calamity which has befallen this generation.

What, then, is it we want when the war is over? I know of no better formula than that more than once made use of, with universal approval, by Mr Asquith in the speeches which he has from time to time delivered. He has repeatedly told his hearers that we are waging war in order to obtain reparation and security. Both are essential, but of the two security is perhaps the more indispensable. In the way of reparation much can no doubt be accomplished, but the utmost effort to make good all the ravages of this war must fall short of completeness, and will fail to undo the grievous wrong which has been done to humanity. It may, however, be possible to make some amends for the inevitable incompleteness of the reparation if the security afforded is, humanly speaking, complete. To end the war honourably would be a great achievement; to prevent the same curse falling upon our children would be a greater achievement still.

This is our avowed aim, and the magnitude of the issue cannot be exaggerated. For, just as this war has been more dreadful than any war in history, so we may be sure would the next war be even more dreadful than this. The prostitution of science for purposes of pure destruction is not likely to stop short. Most of us, however, believe that it should be possible to secure posterity against the repetition of such an outrage as that of 1914. If the Powers will, under a solemn pact, bind themselves to submit future disputes to arbitration; if they will undertake to outlaw, politically and economically, any one of their number which refuses to enter into such a pact, or to use their joint military and naval forces for the purpose of coercing a Power which breaks away from the rest, they will, indeed, have travelled far along the road which leads to security.

We are, at any rate, right to put security in the front line of our peace demands, and it is not unsatisfactory to note that in principle there seems to be complete unanimity upon this point.

In his speech at the banquet of the League to Enforce Peace, on 28 May 1916, President Wilson spoke strongly in favour of:

A universal association of nations … to prevent any war from being begun either contrary to treaty covenants or without warning and full submission of the cause to the opinion of the world.

Later in the same year the German Chancellor, at the sitting of the Main Committee of the Reichstag, used the following language:

> When, as after the termination of the war, the world will fully recognise its horrible devastation of blood and treasure, then through all mankind will go the cry for peaceful agreements and understandings which will prevent, so far as is humanly possible, the return of such an immense catastrophe. This cry will be so strong and so justified that it must lead to a result. Germany will honourably co-operate in investigating every attempt to find a practical solution and collaborate towards its possible realisation.

The Papal Note communicated to the Powers in August last places in the front rank:

> The establishment of arbitration on lines to be concerted and with sanction to be settled against any State that refuses either to submit international disputes to arbitration or to accept its awards.

This suggestion was immediately welcomed by the Austrian Government, which declared that it was conscious of the importance for the promotion of peace of the method proposed by his Holiness, viz., 'to submit international disputes to compulsory arbitration', and that it was prepared to enter into negotiations regarding this proposal. Similar language was used by Count Czernin, the Austro-Hungarian Foreign Minister, in his declaration on foreign policy made at Budapest in October, when he mentioned as one of the 'fundamental bases' of peace that, of 'obligatory international arbitration'.

In his despatch covering the Allied Note of 10 January 1917, Mr Balfour mentions as one of the three conditions essential to a durable peace the condition that:

> Behind international law and behind all treaty arrangements for preventing or limiting hostilities some form of international sanction might be devised which would give pause to the hardiest aggressor.

Such sanction would probably take the form of coercion applied in one of two modes. The 'aggressor' would be disciplined either by the pressure of superior naval and military strength, or by the denial of commercial access and facilities.

The proceedings of the Paris Conference show that we should not shrink from such a denial, if we were compelled to use the weapon for purposes of self-defence. But while a commercial 'boycott' would be justifiable as a war measure, and while the threat of a 'boycott', in case Germany should show herself utterly unreasonable, would be a legitimate threat, no reasonable man would, surely, desire to destroy the trade of the Central Powers, if they will, so to speak, enter into recognisances to keep the peace, and do not force us into conflict by a hostile combination. Commercial war is less ghastly in its immediate results than the war of armed forces, but it would be deplorable if after three or four years of sanguinary conflict in the field, a conflict which has destroyed a great part of the wealth of the world, and permanently crippled its resources, the Powers were to embark upon commercial hostilities certain to retard the economic recovery of all the nations involved.

That we shall have to secure ourselves against the fiscal hostility of others, that we shall have to prevent the recurrence of the conditions under which, when war broke out, we found ourselves short of essential commodities, because we had allowed certain industries, and certain sources of supply, to pass entirely under the control of our enemies, no one will doubt, subject however to this reservation, that it will surely be for our interest that the stream of trade should, so far as our own fiscal interests permit, be allowed to flow strong and interrupted to its natural channels.

There remains the question of territorial claims. The most authoritative statement of these is to be found in the Allies' Note of 10 January 1917. This statement must obviously be regarded as broad outline of the desiderata of the Allies, but is anyone prepared to argue that the sketch is complete, or that it may not become necessary to re-examine it?

Mr Asquith, speaking at Liverpool in October last, used the following language:

> No one pretends that it would be right or opportune for either side to formulate an ultimatum, detailed, exhaustive, precise, with clauses and sub-clauses, which is to be accepted *verbatim et literatim*, chapter and verse, as the indispensable preliminary and condition of peace.

'There are many things,' he added, 'in a worldwide conflict such as this, which must of necessity be left over for discussion and negotiation, for accommodation and adjustment, at a later stage.'

It is surely most important that this wise counsel should be kept in mind. Some of our original desiderata have probably become unattainable. Others would probably now be given a less prominent place than when they were first put forward. Others, again, notably the reparation due to Belgium, remain, and must always remain, in the front rank, but when it comes to the wholesale rearrangement of the map of south-eastern Europe we may well ask for a suspension of judgment and for the elucidation which a frank exchange of views between the Allied Powers can alone afford.

For all these questions concern our Allies as well as ourselves, and if we are to have an Allied Council for the purpose of adapting our strategy in the field to the ever-shifting developments of the war, it is fair to assume that, in the matter of peace terms also, the Allies will make it their business to examine, and if necessary to revise, the territorial requirements.

Let me end by explaining why I attach so much importance to these considerations. We are not going to lose this war, but its prolongation will spell ruin for the civilised world, and an infinite addition to the load of human suffering which already weighs upon it. Security will be invaluable to a world which has the vitality to profit by it, but what will be the value of the blessings of peace to nations so exhausted that they can scarcely stretch out a hand with which to grasp them?

On my belief, if the war is to be brought to a close in time to avert a worldwide catastrophe, it will be brought to a close because on both sides the peoples of the countries involved realise that it has already lasted too long.

There can be no question that this feeling prevails extensively in Germany, Austria and Turkey. We know beyond doubt that the economic pressure in those countries far exceeds any to which we are subject here. Ministers inform us in their speeches of 'constant efforts' on the part of the Central Powers 'to initiate peace talk'. (Sir E. Geddes at the Mansion House, 9 November.)

If the peace talk is not more articulate, and has not been so precise as to enable His Majesty's Government to treat it seriously, the explanation is probably to be found in the fact that first, that German despotism does not tolerate independent expressions of opinion, and second, that the German Government has contrived, probably with success, to misrepresent the aims of the Allies, which are supposed to include the destruction of Germany, the imposition upon her of a form of government decided by her enemies, her destruction as a great commercial community, and her exclusion from the free use of the seas.

An immense stimulus would probably be given to the peace party in Germany if it were understood:

1. That we do not desire the annihilation of Germany as a Great Power;

2. That we do not seek to impose upon her people any form of government other than that of their own choice;

3. That, except as a legitimate war measure, we have no desire to deny to Germany her place among the great commercial communities of the world;

4. That we are prepared, when the war is over, to examine in concert with other Powers the group of international problems, some of them of recent origin, which are connected with the question of 'the freedom of the seas';

5. That we are prepared to enter into an international pact under which ample opportunities would be afforded for the settlement of international disputes by peaceful means.

I am under the impression that authority could be found for most of these propositions in Ministerial speeches. Since the above lines were written, 1, 2 and 3 have been dealt with by our own Foreign Minister at the public meeting held in honour of M. Venizelos at the Mansion House.

The question of the 'freedom of the seas' was amongst those raised at the outset by our American Allies. The formula is an ambiguous one, capable of many inconsistent interpretations, and I doubt whether it will be seriously contended that there is no room for profitable discussion.

That an attempt should be made to bring about the kind of pact suggested in 5 is, I believe, common ground to all the belligerents, and probably to all the neutral Powers.

If it be once established that there are no insurmountable difficulties in the way of agreement upon these points, the political horizon might perhaps be scanned with better hope by those who pray, but can at this moment hardly venture to expect, that a new year may bring us a lasting and honourable peace.

I am, Sir, your obedient servant,

Lansdowne
Lansdowne House

ALLIED WAR AIMS

Lord Lansdowne's Letter

SIR – Lord Lansdowne's hostile critics, almost without exception, write as if the policy he advocates implied a weakening of the will to fight. To argue thus is, intentionally or unintentionally, to beg the whole question. This nation, like others, has suffered intolerable wrong from Germany, and is threatened with intolerable danger in the future, therefore we fight, have fought, and mean to go on fighting until we see our way to some degree of 'reparation and security'. The whole nation is involved; the whole nation, with infinitesimal exceptions, is working and making sacrifices. So far we are all agreed. The question is whether we shall fight and work less well, or be less ready to make sacrifices, if we know what object we are fighting for and recognise that object to be both just and moderate. For myself, as an average man, I know I shall do my modest part in the war much better and with better heart. I have never for a moment begun to lose heart about these matters except when reading certain articles or listening to certain speeches which – so I am credibly informed – were intended as war propaganda to rouse my fighting spirit. I looked askance at some Socialist working men whom I saw near me, and devoutly hoped they were asleep. But I fear they were not and I wondered what our rulers thought men were made of.

In one place only is Lord Lansdowne's letter likely to damp the fighting spirit. It will doubtless do so in Germany and Austria, if the enemy Governments allow it to circulate there, but I fear that is not likely. What the enemy Governments want their subjects to believe is the exact opposite of Lord Lansdowne's five points: that we do wish to destroy Germany and impose upon her an English-appointed Government; that we do mean, unconditionally, to strangle German trade, and to make of the League of Nations a vast anti-German alliance, which shall reduce the peoples of central Europe to a state resembling serfdom, such as the worst pan-Germans proposed for France; and, lastly, that we absolutely refuse to discuss any international problems, whether relating to sea power or otherwise. Put forward that programme, and I do not know if it will make anyone in England fight the better, but it will certainly rally the Germans round the Kaiser and earn the gratitude of the Berlin Press Bureau.

Yours obediently,
Gilbert Murray
Oxford

SIR – To reply to Lord Lansdowne's letter in detail would occupy too much of your space, but one matter must be emphasised in the nation's interest for the sake of all those thousands of men who have gallantly laid down their lives in our own and the Allied cause. Lord Lansdowne is absolutely right when he says that we are fighting for one thing above all – security. Security against the repetition of such a horror as this war, which has deluged the whole world with blood. But what security does he suggest? Germany's word – Germany's solemn pact. As M. Clemenceau has lately remarked, the Belgians, looking at their desolated country, can tell us what Germany's pledges are worth.

The decisive defeat of Germany is essential, for since it is impossible to trust her promises, the only possible safeguard for Europe is to be found in her powerlessness. The other word must be added. Lord Lansdowne says that we do not wish to force upon the German people a form of government which is objectionable to them. That is true. Such an attempt would be futile in any case, seeing the permanent conquest of Germany is and never has been any part of the Allied programme. But the fact remains and should not be ignored that so long as the despotic hate of the Hohenzollerns continues, so long will the whole of Europe need to stand on guard against Germany's aggressiveness. Whether a democratic Germany is possible, and whether, if a democratic Germany did come into existence, it would prove less aggressive than the autocracy which the German nation has hitherto so whole-heartedly supported in all its crimes, the future only can show. I am not myself sanguine, but if as some hopeful people think, the Germans are capable of reform, the best and undoubtedly the only proof they can offer would be the overthrow, complete and final, of their present rulers.

Yours faithfully,
E. Bowden-Smith, Hon. Sec.
British Empire Union, 346 Strand, W.C.2

————

17 December 1917

CHRISTMAS SHOPPING

SIR – In the interests of a large community – the shopkeepers and assistants of the country – may we appeal through your columns to the public to make their Christmas purchases as early as possible in the week remaining before Yuletide, and early in the day. Leaving purchases to the last day and hour is trying to the sellers at any time, but more particularly so when shops and establishments are working under special difficulties.

Faithfully yours,

Winston Churchill, President
E. Cubitt Sayers, Chairman
G.J. Bentham, Parliamentary Chairman
Albert Larking, Secretary
Early Closing Association, 34–40, Ludgate Hill, E.C.4

3 January 1918

WOMEN TRANSPORT DRIVERS

SIR – May I draw the attention of your readers to the very urgent need of more women motor transport drivers? The services of so many women are required for this purpose in the Royal Flying Corps that I am anxious to appeal to all women who are suitable to volunteer for this national work. Applicants must have driving experience and be willing to serve where required in the United Kingdom. Application should be made to the Commandant, Women's Legion Motor Transport Section, 13a Pall Mall East, S.W.1

Yours, &c.,

Londonderry
Londonderry House, Park Lane, W.1

———

THE AIR IN 1918

SIR – After upwards of three years' war in the air it might not be out of place to consider what has been done and what can still be done by properly directed effort. For the past, we may sum up everything in one sentence – the blunders of our politicians have been retrieved by the heroism of our aviators. It was this heroism and marvellous courage, coupled with the supreme fighting instinct of our youthful 'air sportsmen', that led our generals (often, I fear, not quite accurately) to claim for us supremacy in the air. This was true so far as the actual individual contests went, but, alas! no real effort was made at home to attain such a command of the air as would paralyse the activities of the German army on the Western Front.

It is clear that in 1917 there has been to a great extent equality of material in the air forces at the front. The very mobility of air power involves temporary supremacy at a given spot at a given time for whichever Power chooses to concentrate. For example, when we were the attacking force, as at Vimy Ridge, Mossines and Cambrai, we had the mastery of the air by reason of the invisible concentration which we had prepared; on the other hand, in the case of the German attacks at Lombartzyde, Italy, and the surprise thrust at Cambrai, the mastery passed temporarily to them, and so it must be until one side or the other, by great and persistent manufacturing effort, can present its generals with an overwhelming number of high-powered machines.

So much for 1917, with its lack of imagination and slackness in manufacture: but what of 1918? War on foot is generally ended by the invasion of the enemy's country. All history from the time of Caesar to the Russo-Japanese War teaches this. May it not be the same in the air? Whichever side can effectively invade the other in the air will win the war. Lord Rothermere, our new Air Minister, has, I am delighted to see, spoken out frankly and courageously as to 'reprisals', which is only another word for aerial invasion, but let us see to it that the invasion is on the right side. Often we have been invaded by squadrons of Gothas up to twenty-five in number. True, only a few have readied London, but are not Essex and Kent equally parts of Britain; and we have at last invaded Germany at Mannheim with eleven machines. I disregard altogether mere tactical raids on Belgian aerodromes. They have nothing to do with a strategic effort to end the war. They are comparable only to the cavalry raids of olden time, and have little more real effect.

What then of the future of this year? The war will probably end before the autumn. Germany can hardly stand another winter, but she will make a desperate effort to win in the air by an invasion of England this summer. If she invades London night after night, as she may do, we shall of course put up gallant defence, but the only way to stop her is a counter-invasion of the Rhine towns. We all revere the heroic defence of Verdun two years ago by our French Allies, but what saved Verdun was our counter-attack on the Somme; and what will save London will be our counter-attack on Cologne. Can we accomplish this? I do not mean petty raids of twenty or thirty machines at intervals of ten days, but a real invasion by 100 machines a day, repeated until the dose cures, or rather kills, the patient. I make no attacks or even criticisms; nor do I state publicly what I know of the manufacturing position. I merely ask, can we do it?

Yours, &c.,

W. Joynson-Hicks

---

5 January 1918

THE AIR IN 1918

SIR – Mr Joynson Hicks has done national service by drawing attention in your columns to the importance of the air service during the year which is just commencing. Germany has enjoyed one great advantage over the Allies, for Germany has appreciated the fact that the present is a war in which science must play a deciding part, and where mere physical bravery is not as important as in the days of old.

This is especially true in connection with the air service. More attention should be concentrated on the design and development of aeroplanes than has been the case during the last three years. The facilities for research in aeronautics should be increased, but this is not all. The bravest man on the best aeroplane ever designed could, without technical knowledge, accomplish little. Yet at the present time the young men who at eighteen or eighteen and a half are admitted to the Flying Corps have as a rule only received the 'general education' provided at the public or secondary schools of the country.

A man who is to become a really efficient pilot should have received before entering the Government service a sound ground in science and in engineering. This fact is fully appreciated by those connected with the Air Council, but the official machine must necessarily move slowly. The only preliminary course specially designed for young men who wish to become pilots in the air service is at the East London College. More facilities for such instruction should be provided.

Even a six-month course such as that alluded to is hardly adequate. A scheme should be devised whereby a combination of special aeronautical training with military instruction is possible. Important as is the design of an aeroplane, the efficiency of the man who is to handle it is no less important.

Yours, &c.,

John L.S. Hatton
East London College, Mile End Road, E.

---

7 January 1918

SOCKS FOR THE TROOPS

SIR – Will you allow me through your paper to thank most sincerely those who so generously responded to my appeal for funds to provide wool for my knitters who are making socks for our soldiers. We have sent out 800 pairs since last August, and have over 400 still to go out, but I have no more wool left now, and socks are ever more and more urgently needed. My knitters, all but one, are voluntary, and many of them working women. They are keen to help, and do splendid work, the blind knitter, to whom I alluded before, having now completed 200 pairs of socks. May I earnestly appeal for more funds to carry on this most necessary work? Wool is getting dearer and dearer. I have the chance to procure a large quantity of excellent wool at a moderate price if only funds are forthcoming at once. The worst weather is still to come, and socks will be needed in ever-increasing quantities.

Yours faithfully,

Evelyn Templetown
10 Onslow Crescent, S.W.7

———

8 January 1918

THE TESTING TIME

SIR – Everyone who is at all sensitive to the signs of the times realises instinctively that Britain has now reached, and during the next six months will be compelled to pass through, one of the gravest crises of her long and varied history. But, though everyone realises it instinctively, it may be well to state the fact explicitly. Britain has now to face, and will during the coming half-year have to contend with, three perils of unprecedented magnitude, viz., first, the peril of Austro-German attack; secondly, the peril of famine; and, thirdly, the peril of her own Bolsheviks. A word as to each.

A year ago the decisive defeat of the Central Empires appeared certain. The Allies on the Western Front were impregnable in defence and strong for attack; the Russians on the Eastern Front, well supplied for the first time with all the munitions of war, had before them a comparatively easy task in the reconquest of Galicia and Poland. Now, however, all the advantages secured by strenuous effort and devoted sacrifice have been recklessly cast away by a band of fanatics whose folly has jeopardised the very cause to which they profess supreme devotion. Hence the certainty of the Allied victory has been converted, not by German strength or prudence, but by the feebleness and lunacy of the Leninites, into the grim necessity for a renewal of desperate conflict to escape disaster. The entry of the United States into the war, happily, more than counterbalances the Russian collapse; but not for some months can the might of America fully display itself, and during that critical interval it will rest with the sorely tried veterans who have already stood the strain of over three years of unparalleled warfare to hold their front intact against what will probably prove to be the most desperate of all the onslaughts of the enemy. Of their ability to do it there is fortunately no doubt, provided only that they are adequately and steadily supported and fortified at home.

We at home, however, are faced with a prospect of famine, more near and formidable than has ever faced the people of this country since the close of the Middle Ages. Shall we pass through our ordeal of hunger with the same serene certainty of success as will our soldiers through their ordeal of fire? We ought to do so; for we shall have to bear nothing worse than the Germans have already borne with exemplary discipline and docility for over two years. It would be an everlasting disgrace to democracy if it could not endure in the cause of its high ideals the hardships to which the slaves who seek for world power patiently submit. But the omens are not wholly good. There are heard in our midst baseless or wildly exaggerated cries of 'profiteering', senseless demands for reductions of prices, ignorant protests against inevitable privations, violent threats in case supplies are not forthcoming. There is thus urgent need that the nation should be told clearly the unpleasant truth, viz., that the customary food is not available on any terms, and that the people should be called to sacrifice and duty.

It is the hardships which must unavoidably be faced by all classes of the community that renders the peril of the British Bolsheviks so grave. Such mistaken people as believe that their hardships are due, not to causes inseparable from the war, but to failure on the part of the Government or to the machinations of 'profiteers', fall an easy prey to pacifists, syndicalists, Germanophiles and other types of Bolshevik agitators, who see in the present discontents a golden opportunity to precipitate the 'social revolution' and the 'class war'. Hence there is need at one and the same time of a vigorous campaign of enlightenment for the people, and of a policy of stern suppression of those who would undermine the nation's resolve to subordinate all personal interests and all party questions to the pursuit of this just and necessary struggle to a conclusion in decisive victory.

For if, but only if, we endure to the end, we shall be saved. Our own fortitude and exertions will baffle the German assaults; the strength of the United States will enable the offensive once more to be undertaken; finally, the better Russia is bound to some extent to recover herself, and when she does so her forces will once more take their stand by the armies of the Allies, and play an important part of the last stages of the war. It is for us, then, to steel ourselves to bear the burden of this critical half-year, to restrict the allurements of ignoble ease and the attractions of a peace to be gained by the surrender of our ideals. It is for us to pursue the great conflict, in the course of which we have already sacrificed so much, until our enemy has been punished for his unspeakable crimes, has been compelled to make reparation to his victims, and has been rendered harmless for the future. Only after a decisive victory over the forces of evil as embodied in the German military autocracy will it be possible to turn with buoyancy and hope to the tasks of domestic reconstruction which the war has placed before us.

Yours, &c.,

F.J.C, Hearnshaw
University of London, King's College, Strand

————

APPEAL FOR WOMEN'S SERVICES

SIR – Some months ago I made a joint appeal in the press, on behalf of the Central Joint VAD Committee, for women to offer their services for the sick and wounded. Once again I have to come to the public with the appeal for personal service in carrying on the work to which we have put our hand. During the last month the number of VAD members posted to meet the demands of the naval and military authorities has been very large, and although members are coming from overseas to help us, we are now in urgent need of nursing members for military and auxiliary hospitals at home and abroad. The Army is recruiting women for its service through the WAAC, and the Navy will shortly be doing so through the WRNS; we appeal for workers in, perhaps, the highest function of women's service, the nursing back to health of the men broke in this world struggle. Recent events have brought before the public questions of which we have never lost sight, such as welfare and reforms in the VAD organisation. Amendments to the Army Council instruction, which deals with general service VAD workers, have been submitted to the military authorities. Co-ordination in both hospital and convalescent treatment for VADs is now near realisation; a central non-residential club for all VADs in uniform is shortly to be opened; the red efficiency stripe will be given responsible duties accordingly. This concession, which we have so long been urging the military authorities to grant, will greatly improve the status of VAD workers in military hospitals.

We have an urgent demand for general service members, cooks, assistant cooks, kitchenmaids, wardmaids and housemaids. We have now sent some hundreds of those general service members to France, there are thousands working in our hospitals at home, and we have reports of the excellent work they are doing. We feel sure that the spirit of the women of this country is strong enough to see this great struggle through to the finish, and this they can best do by offering a yet further share of that splendid unswerving service which has characterised the work of the VADs throughout the war. It is a great work, which does not come into the limelight, but its glory is, perhaps, the greater by reason of the very fact that it does not obtrude. Without new workers the strain will be almost too great for those who are now giving their services; a large response to this appeal will help to bring us within sight of the end for which we all long. Applications for either nursing or general VAD service should be addressed to the Chairman, VAD Department, Devonshire House, Piccadilly, London W.1

Yours faithfully,

Arthur Stanley, Chairman
83 Pall Mall, S.W.1

————

9 January 1918

BRITISH MUSEUM

What Removal Means

SIR – The Government still contemplates the annexation of the British Museum for the Air Board offices; that this action would imperil the nation's heirlooms has been sufficiently discussed in the press; this monstrous and senseless proposition has caused widespread consternation. The clubs in Pall Mall, the Albert Hall, with their possibilities of temporary buildings in the neighbouring parks, each would afford more modern and convenient housing for the Air Board now and after the war.

To speak of the removal of the British Museum treasures in two months, makes one shudder at the practical sense of the new Air Board. With the expert labour available before the war such a work of removal and rehousing would have taken nine months or more. Assuming that the really national service of protecting our public inheritance of masterpieces were honestly contemplated by the Government, and resourceful Navy men put at the disposal of the British Museum officials (this suggestion allows for the impossible), the dangerous work of removal would take four or six months. There remains one point not hitherto discussed. The duties of the Air Board would not cease with the war, and the British Museum would remain in their hands and closed to the public for years after its termination. The trustees of the British Museum have so far been so apathetic in their public trust that the press alone can urge upon these gentlemen and our overworked Ministers the disastrous character of the proposition to endanger the national heirlooms and the world-famous library. Let the Museum benefit by the suggestion that efficient precaution is to be taken, at last, to save its contents, and let the Air Board find a more practical setting for its proposed improvements in activity and foresight anywhere but near the library of the British Museum.

Yours obediently,

C. Ricketts
Lansdowne House, Lansdowne Road, Holland Park

———

16 January 1918

GLOVES FOR THE WOUNDED

SIR – At this season of the year, when the cold strikes sharply home even in the case of the most robust, surely more might be done for the comfort of the men in hospital whose vitality has been lowered by wounds or sickness. I allude more particularly to such men as are able to go out for daily walks, and to the failure of the authorities to issue those men with warm gloves as part of their regular hospital kit. It may, of course, be answered that if the men find their hands cold, they can put them in their overcoat pockets; but in the first place, this is a sloppy and unsoldierlike practice, which does not make for brisk walking, and should not be encouraged; and in the second place, it must be remembered that for many men it is a physical impossibility, as they have to use crutches or sticks or carry their arms in a sling. It is not a pleasant sight in this, the fourth year of the war, to see a man with three gold stripes on his sleeve toiling painfully up a hill on crutches, with his hands blue with the cold. One can take such a man into the nearest shop and buy him a pair of gloves, but a matter like this is not one for haphazard private benevolence, which may relieve one case, but must perforce leave a hundred thousand unrelieved. It is a matter for action by the War Office. The Red Cross manage to provide the majority of the walking-out patients in, I believe, most of their hospitals with gloves, but there is no general free issue of gloves by Government to men in hospital; they are left to buy them for themselves – out of their 1s 6d a day!

Surely, to put it on the lowest grounds, those of economy, it would be worthwhile to issue all walking-out cases in military hospitals with gloves. Men whose hands are uncomfortably cold gravitate inevitably indoors – back to the hospital, to stuffy, smoke-laden cinemas, or to other, even less desirable, places of amusement – instead of walking about outdoors and getting the exercise and fresh air which would accelerate their recovery, and take them off the non-effective list. The glove issue would only be needed for six and a half months in the year, say from 1 October to 15 April, and if leather gloves with warm lining were obtained, though the initial cost would be greater, it would probably be cheaper in the end, as the gloves would wear better, and would be passed on from case to case.

Yours, &c.,

G.S. Meiklejohn
Hampstead

———

6 February 1918

IRELAND AND CONSCRIPTION

SIR – In these times of stress, when all realise that there are reasons for what the Government do and for what they do not do, we hesitate to recommend action even in matters that seem to be beyond question. With regard to conscription in Ireland, surely no such qualification can apply. Ireland is part of the United Kingdom, and it is monstrous that it should be the only part that should be exempt from compulsory military service in time of Empire peril. Some say that we should wait until the Convention has closed its sittings. The Convention, I understand, is to decide the form of Government for Ireland, and is not to decide how Ireland and the rest of the kingdom can win the war. Unless we have the necessary increase in man power we shall lose it, and if we lose the war it does not matter very much what form of Government the Irish Convention decides upon. On the other hand, we have to remember that in the rest of the United Kingdom the 'comb' is busily at work, and Englishmen, Scotschmen and Welshmen who are called upon to make great personal sacrifices for their country will respond infinitely more readily if Ireland was placed upon an equal footing. To my thinking, at any rate, it is so urgent a question that I trust that all who agree with me will help to make the petition which is being promoted by the National Party for Conscription in Ireland a striking revelation of the real will of the people of the country. Fortified by the knowledge that the whole nation is in favour of equality of sacrifice, I feel sure that the Government would act strongly and take the necessary steps. I am told that some tens of thousands of petition forms are in the hands of voluntary workers throughout the country, and I hope that everyone who shares my views on this matter will write to the Secretary, the National Party, 22 King Street, St James's, S.W.1, and set to work to help make an end of an anomaly which, if it be persisted in, will be fraught with peril to the Empire, and a lasting shame to Ireland herself.

Yours, &c.,
Leconfield
Petworth House, Petworth

TREATMENT OF WOUNDED

SIR – My attention has been drawn to Mr Smallwood's recent speech in the House of Commons, and I note with pleasure his generous reference to the YMCA. It is because I am afraid some points of his speech may give rise to misapprehension that I venture to intervene in this discussion. It is obviously difficult for the War Office to make regulations so as to ensure every case being dealt with as the very natural and proper sentiment may demand, and I believe that is one of the reasons that have led the military authorities to give such ample facilities to the YMCA for carrying on its humanising work at home and overseas. Though absolutely unofficial, the YMCA is to all intents and purposes an unofficial department of the military machine. It is in camp by the courtesy of the military, and all we do is done with the consent, and often at the suggestion, of the military authorities and its representatives.

Another great humanising element within the military machine is the medical and hospital organisation – RAMC, or Red Cross. No doubt mistakes are made at times – it is inevitable when operations are carried out on such a huge scale – but everywhere I hear nothing but praise and appreciation of the kindness and consideration shown by the doctors, nurses and attendants alike. We have every reason to be proud of them. Miss Brown, the lady superintendent of one of our big hostels for the relatives of the dangerously wounded men, wrote to me on 25 January, saying that her attention had been drawn to Mr Smallwood's statement in the House, and she had since discovered that it was one of the hospitals in the neighbourhood in which she was working to which he referred. She adds:

I feel I am in a position to speak on the matter, as I have been here two years on the 14th of next month, and have had over 2,400 visitors and relatives of wounded in my charge. I speak entirely from the relatives' point of view, as I am seldom in the hospitals myself, and they speak very freely and always of the utmost kindness and consideration shown to them and their boys by all in the hospitals and on the journey. Their gratitude has been unbounded. Their treatment has been so different to anything they imagined possible under the circumstances, and again and again have I heard the assertion, even when they have lost their boys, that nothing more could have been done, no hospital at home could have better cared for them, and the patience and tact of both doctors and nurses has amazed them. Again and again has the tap at my window come in the night, which means send a relative along, the boy is worse, and again and again have they been kept the night at the hospital. Of course, there have been cases where absolute quiet was the only chance of recovery, and they have been told to leave the patient, and they have recognised and complied at once with the need. My experience is not only of the five hospitals at our doors, but also during the first sixteen or seventeen months of many other hospitals in the area, and the report has always been to the same effect. I think the true facts should somehow be made known to the people, for in the matter of caring for the wounded the soulless War Office has shown itself especially very kind and human. The nation is at war today, and therefore everyone is concerned for their men, and nothing is too much to be done for them, but the whole truth, as a whole, not an isolated case for which there may be a special reason for special treatment, should be quoted ...

I sympathise deeply with Mr Smallwood, but think it only fair to the devoted people who run our hospitals, as well as to the military authorities, to make this communication to the press.

Your obedient servant,
Arthur K. Yapp
YMCA, W.1

---

4 June 1918

SHORTAGE OF ACCOUNTANTS

SIR – It is admitted by everyone who knows the circumstances that at the present time there is almost a famine of qualified accountants and it is needless to labour this fact in the face of the revelations exposed lately in Ministry of Munitions, and so short is the country of accountants it has been found necessary to recall as many as possible from the combatant ranks, and also to obtain help from abroad, while there are also special instructions issued to tribunals with regard to their indispensability and exemption. The consequence is, that many young and healthy men of military age have of necessity been kept out of the fighting ranks. I do not for a moment question the wisdom of this step, for if there is to be any proper control of the enormous expenditure now going on it can only be checked by those qualified to deal with it. What I desire to suggest is that the Government should take steps to try and remedy this shortage by offering special facilities and opportunities to wounded soldiers and other suitable candidates to acquire this special knowledge by means of training schools under the administration of qualified accountants. I would particularly emphasise the opportunity that would thus be offered to wounded soldiers with an aptitude for figures of acquiring a profession of great value to them after the war. In the training I suggest, frequent examinations should be held, to test the progress of the candidates, and if a candidate is found wanting in the necessary aptitude he should not be retained.

Trained accountants will be required just as much to clear up the aftermath of the war as now, while with the expansion of trade which is to be expected when the war is over the opportunities for employment should be much increased. It will be argued by the 'trade unions' in the accountancy profession that it is impossible to make a qualified accountant without years of training and experience, but the war has shown the fallacy of most preconceived ideas – gunners and airmen can now be trained in a few months, and even Cabinet Ministers have risen from obscurity in the course of a year or so. Therefore, why cannot qualified accountants be made within a reasonable time, given the opportunity of training?

Yours faithfully,
G. Bettesworth-Piggott, Deputy-Chairman, Appeal Tribunal,
House of Commons

5 November 1918

WHEN WE TALK OF PEACE

SIR – As I read the brilliant pen-picture written by your correspondent Mr H.C. Bailey on the 'Great Advance' this 'question presented itself to my mind'. 'Always,' he says, 'when we talk of peace let us remember that belt of desert forty miles broad, and remember that the men who willed and ordered its desolation have boasted of it and gloried in it as one of the triumphs of the German war.' Stretch county upon county as long and as deep as Sussex, picture towns and hamlets bashed to pieces, plough and pasture churned with shell, untillable for a generation, woods and coverts stripped and shattered, and then you get some little idea of what France and Belgium have endured. Desolation of desolation such as Daniel the prophet never dreamed of. Some day a less squeamish authority will tell what the daughters of those countries have endured, and the women and maidens in this country may thank God for their island home, their fleet and armies. They were saved on the high seas and on the fields of Flanders. The women have the vote. Trade union leaders have toured some of these districts. Send women, young women from every county and every town in the United Kingdom, from the Greater Britains beyond the seas, from every state in the United States, from all neutral countries, organise these parties officially, let the states pay the expense, let armies of them be taken over the shell-shattered soil of France, that they may tell their children's children of the Hell of the Hun. I don't want the tea-gossipers of the West End alone to go.

I want the women from every class to see these things. Then they will know what war is in all its fearful brutality. Seeing is believing, and there is precious little imagination in a hard-working labourer's cottage or a working man's tenement. Let the women from neutral countries, whether from Spain, Scandinavia or South America, see and hear in France and Belgium what hell on earth is. The seamen know in every Allied and neutral state, and their vengeance is deep. Vainly will a German ship call for aid. But the women of the world cannot realise the sufferings of France and Belgium until they gaze on their scarred and wounded soils. Let women visit the war zone, let them come from the four quarters of the world as soon as time and circumstances permit. They will understand why their menfolk fought and died. This war may then end war.

Your obedient servant,

Templar

---

7 *November 1918*

THE ENEMY'S DESTRUCTION

SIR – Thousands of women will endorse unreservedly the excellent letter of 'Templar' in today's *Daily Telegraph*, urging that parties of women should go to France in order to learn by actual fact the terrible meaning of war. But while any little group of men are granted all facilities to see what our armies have accomplished and the deliverance that has been wrought, such privileges have been constantly and persistently withheld from women. May I remind you, sir, that in August last Sir Harry Brittain suggested in your own columns that a representative party of women munition workers and aircraft workers should be sent out, that they might see for themselves what their handicraft had achieved in the liberation of Belgium and northern France. The suggestion enjoyed your own powerful support, and Sir Robert Hadfield generously offered a hundred guineas if desirable towards the expenses. I understand that the scheme was viewed with approval in high official quarters, but it was passed on to the War Aims Committee, who have done nothing in the matter, and who should be compelled by public opinion to make some movement.

The General Election is close upon us, the women's vote will be of vast importance, and nothing would have greater influence towards a sternly just settlement when peace can be discussed than a realisation of the unspeakable crimes and wanton destruction wrought by the German invaders. There is a strong feeling among working women that their reasonable claims to recognition are being overlooked, and that as taxpayers and voters they have the right to see something of what their labours have contributed to the naval and military triumphs that have been won. 'The prospect now before us has been made possible by the women of the country,' said Mrs Lloyd George at the City Temple, on Monday evening. There is no reason whatever why parties of women selected by the votes of their sister workers in the factories should not start next week. Accommodation can be arranged for them in the camps of

Queen Mary's Army Auxiliary Corps, and the minor details would not need an hour's arrangement.

I am, Sir, yours obediently,

Working Woman
London